MAKE A NEW SOUND

£4.30

BY THE SAME AUTHOR

New Sounds in Class
Aural Adventures

GEORGE SELF

Principal Lecturer in Music at La Sainte Union College, Southampton

Make a New Sound

UNIVERSAL EDITION

Contents

Introduction

It is difficult to believe that George Self's *New Sounds in Class* appeared for the first time as recently as 1967. The climate then and the changes that have occurred since that time have been so rapid and far-reaching that it seems much longer ago than it really is. To say that this earlier publication was a milestone in the progress of music in education, not only in this country but in many parts of the world, would be a modest assessment of its value. Although only a slender volume, it effectively redirected the attention of many teachers and caused them to focus their thoughts in a way that encouraged them to use their own powers of imagination, and those of their pupils, in approaching the music of the present. The exercise was essentially a practical one and one that was easily accessible to everyone because it appealed directly to the innate musical qualities that exist in human nature. This is not to say, however, that the roots were not sturdy and the philosophy deep as well as eminently clear. The opening essay on 'Music in the Twentieth Century' provides ample evidence of this, and is still one of the most valuable short introductions to the subject that appears in print. The considerable extension of resources that has been made available since the appearance of this essay must alone serve as an indication of the progress made during the intervening years. There is still a great deal of ground to be covered, however, before music can achieve the full role that it is capable of fulfilling in the scheme of education.

The primary aim of *Make a New Sound* is to provide readers with a collection of ideas for group work that is based on performance, composition, and improvisation in a way that encourages individuals to make use of their technical and creative skills in a developing programme. It is the members of the group who decide the rules within which they will operate: the intensity of experience possible within this framework is likely to prove much more satisfying than most of that which they could achieve in simply performing works that provide an almost completely prescribed situation in which they have very little opportunity to make imaginative contributions of their own. By relating music to art, movement, and number, and exploring the resources that become available through the use of electronic equipment, forms emerge that enable the group to maintain control of the medium while at the same time retaining maximum flexibility and the sense of deep involvement that can only come from feeling one's way along a largely unpredetermined path. A living world of music is produced in which the participants are able to enjoy moments of aesthetic and emotional discovery that are unlike any other, and expressive of inner feelings well beyond the power of words. They become directly involved in the process of composition, which, far from detracting from more traditional approaches to music-making, must surely complement them and add to their effectiveness by sharpening perception and intensifying response; always assuming, of course, that these approaches are such as to be worth pursuing at all. If dull, lethargic, rote-singing lessons, linked with a view of notational theory that is divorced from practice and supplemented by dictated notes on the life of this or that composer, has been the order of the day, it is to be hoped that the introduction of some of the elements in this book will help to change the course of the work completely. It is hardly possible to offer enrichment to a course that is by its very nature antipathetic to begin with. Where really lively musical work already exists, however, an opportunity is provided here to redress the balance between creative and recreative activities as well as between the music of the present and that of the past. The considerable extension of resources that has become available in recent years is also put to effective use.

By encouraging the assimilation of general principles from within easily accessible musical experiences rather than pursuing narrow paths in a detailed and detached manner, it is possible to relate music-making directly to the sound environment of today, employing initially those skills of voice and hand already possessed by each individual. As awareness of rhythm, pitch, timbre and amplitude grows through this experience, so will awareness of deficiencies in ability to control these elements encourage the desire to achieve the technical skill that is necessary to manipulate them in a more detailed fashion. Similarly, longer forms of expression will lead to a felt need for some kind of notation to aid an already improved quality of musical memory.

Although the forms of notation devised may sometimes bear little obvious resemblance to conventional notation, this too will take on a new significance as the purposeful nature of its function becomes clearer, and it is seen as a practical resource rather than an ambiguous collection of symbols that relates only to the past. Such a procedure as has been outlined allows for great variation in the capacity of individuals. It enables them to operate effectively in group activities that enjoy a wide range of possibility; it also constitutes the most valid reason of all for developing performing and notational techniques by creating a situation in which the pupil wants to develop them because he feels an immediate need to add to his ability in order to express himself. If all this is seen as an extension of a process that begins at birth, the role of the teacher is clearly one that is concerned with complementing natural forces in such a way as to encourage the healthy growth of individual personalities through aesthetic and emotional experiences that relate also to the development of social sense and self-discipline. Nothing could be further from the confused and often irrelevant imposition of preordained patterns that still sometimes passes as the teaching of music. Where such practices exist, it is hardly surprising that the result is often apathy, open rebellion, or a situation where young people prefer to educate themselves rather than submit to something with which they have little sympathy or sense of identity. Indeed, the almost obsessional pursuit of music that goes on outside the classroom makes it difficult to accept as reasonable, or even comprehensible, that it is not possible to do more to harness and develop educationally a driving force of such intensity. If the materialistically motivated pop-music industry is capable of the stimulation and control that is apparent, it must surely be within the capacity of those concerned with education to develop the spiritual and aesthetic qualities that are so obviously inherent in this impressive flow of energy.

In compiling an introduction such as this it would be inappropriate to indulge in a series of anecdotes about the author, unless such references have direct bearing on the work itself. That George Self is in fact a somewhat reluctant author does have such a bearing, for his reluctance reflects a personality that is concerned with moving forward from the present. What was done yesterday has already become history and he has no wish to stop or be held back from the immense flow of creative energy that carries him along. He is concerned with what is happening now and what can be caused to happen next. His concern is expressed in a boundless enthusiasm and a zest for life that manifests itself through musical activities, interwoven with an insight into educational processes that achieves a remarkable degree of depth, clarity, and simplicity. To know this is to know that nothing could be further from his mind than to have produced, in this book, anything so puerile as a method that is to be followed slavishly in the order in which it is presented. The sections are mostly self-contained and may therefore be read in many suitable orders; their contents are intended to serve as a stimulus to the imagination of the reader and to encourage him to devise ways of creating that are beyond, as well as within, the boundaries of these pages. The development of a divergent attitude of mind through creative activity is likely to act more effectively as a corrective to a basically convergent society than any amount of verbosity and any number of palliative gestures.

Ormskirk, April 1973   VICTOR PAYNE

This book is the outcome of some of the work done with school pupils and college students in the years 1966 to 1972.

                                                         GEORGE SELF

Acknowledgements

Thanks are due to Mary Davies for granting permission to incorporate her long picture into the cover design. The four smaller paintings, shown on the back cover, are by Elizabeth McClosky and other past students of La Sainte Union College of Education in Southampton.

We are grateful also to Peter Hutchings for allowing us to use an extract from his *Jabberwocky* (Chapter 3 Ex. 12), to Philip Ellis for his vocal piece (Chapter 3 Ex. 14), and Sr. M. Gabriel O.S.U. for the extract from her *Pensive Mood* (Chapter 6 Ex. 12).

Cover layout design by Barry Atkinson

More New Sounds Nos. 1-3 are available separately in the *Music for Young Players* series.

ORDER OUT OF CHAOS

(A large gathering, each person with some sound-source — woodwind, brass, bowed strings, plucked strings, tuned percussion, untuned percussion, home-made, ready-made . . .)

Sound/silence

Instruction: 'Play (anything!) on the first signal, make the sound cease on the second.' The players begin as required and on the second signal they stop playing — but some of the instruments go on sounding and all do not seem to be aware of this. Some of the players even talk, having found nothing to listen to in this wonderful variety of sound.

The instruction is repeated, this time with the addition: 'Listen intently immediately after the second signal to sounds that you hear inside and outside the room.' This time, or next time, players with metallophones, chime-bars, guitars, autoharps, and so on, realize that 'to make the sound cease' requires a *positive* action — hand-damping and not mere cessation of playing. (Does this mean that we have formerly heard no distinction between, say, a melody played on a flute and the same melody played with the sounds overlapping on chime-bars, or that we have not heard chords I, IV and V intermingled on metallophones? Has pedalling at the change of chord on the piano been mechanically remembered as a rule, or as something required by the ear? Do the hands remain on the keys of the piano at the end of a phrase? Does the choir cease singing at the end of a piece just when it feels like it?) What do we hear in the 'silence' — a cough, breathing, creaking of chairs, a vacuum cleaner in the corridor, a bird singing, wind howling, rain on the windows, a car changing gear, an aeroplane, the fans of the heating system? Many of these sounds we hear together in a random and fascinating counterpoint — why compose when these sounds occur in such amazing orders and combinations? Have these sounds more interest than those deliberately organized by man? Does listening to them create in us a desire to experiment with the ordering of sounds in new ways?

DEVELOPING A SOUND/SILENCE PIECE

Two basic approaches are possible. *Either* (a) the progress of the piece is precisely timed in seconds, employing signals from a conductor at each change, or the performers observe the passage of time on a clock with a large second-hand;* *or* (b) the conductor ignores clock-time and makes changes from sound to silence and vice versa

Ex. 1

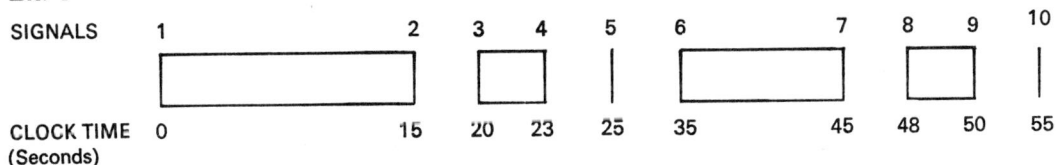

| SIGNALS | 1 | | 2 | 3 | 4 | 5 | 6 | | 7 | 8 | 9 | 10 |

| CLOCK TIME (Seconds) | 0 | | 15 | 20 | 23 | 25 | 35 | | 45 | 48 | 50 | 55 |

---

* The Cantabrian Battery-operated clock, London Instrument Co. Ltd, Newnham Mill, Cambridge, is highly suitable.

1

as he desires — the conductor being, as always, the chief listener. How long are the 'silences'? Does the sound-interest in the 'silence' contrast with that in the musicians' sound? Does it continue this sound in an unexpected manner? The 'silence' lengths will be decided by the conductor with such ideas in mind.

Now attention must be given to the musicians' sound. Was it in fact chaotic? Did a drummer beat out the same rhythm at the same volume, with the same type of beater during each period of playing? Did the melodic percussion players perform only on the white notes? Did the violinist play high notes, low notes, with the bow, *staccato*, *legato*, near the bridge, over the finger-board, *pizzicato*? Did the pianist use the pedal, play on the keyboard, pluck the strings, use beaters on the strings, and so on?

The sound–silence piece is attempted again, with the instruction that each player shall make some change in his performance at each new section (unless, of course, a section is so fascinating that conductor and players wish to recapture the sound).

Perhaps little more variety results than before. Players should be asked not to limit themselves to conventional sequences and ways of playing that they have already learnt, but they should be asked to use their instruments as might a small child at first attempt, were he to be equipped with the dexterity that older people possess (for additional help in overcoming inhibitions in the way of attack, see the next chapter, on Transcription).

After the conductor has pointed out any interesting features of the improvisation, another attempt can be made, the players being asked to react to other interesting sounds made in the group (not necessarily involving mimicry), as well as making each section different in quality.

Is the result now better? Would the sounds heard randomly during 'silence' be more satisfying if they were consciously re-arranged by a composer with the aid of a tape-recorder?

Having achieved some variety, we must now proceed to think of ways in which the performers may be limited in what they do. A composer is always aware of some limits or rules before he composes, because such limits help to define the character of a piece. Elements are dealt with separately, and although of course a composer is conscious of all elements, he may leave some to chance.

Tone-colour

Tone-colour is one of the most important elements, especially in work with children; for tone-colours, if suitably organized, make a framework within which some degree of success is guaranteed. Although it is not possible to equate strings, woodwind and percussion with red, yellow, blue, and so on, tone-colour does play a part in music somewhat related to that of colour in the visual arts.

One of the simplest ways of making a short piece, taking only tone-colour into account, is to make use of a Veitch diagram. Such a diagram may be used to indicate all possible combinations of tone-colour, with the added advantage that many different orders of sections may be used from the one diagram.

Ex. 2

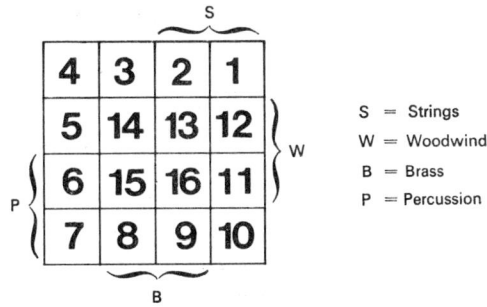

4	3	2	1
5	14	13	12
6	15	16	11
7	8	9	10

S = Strings
W = Woodwind
B = Brass
P = Percussion

If, for example, squares are taken in the order indicated in the diagram above, all possible combinations of S, W, B, P will be heard (including the combination of no instruments at all) in the order shown in the score below:

Ex. 3

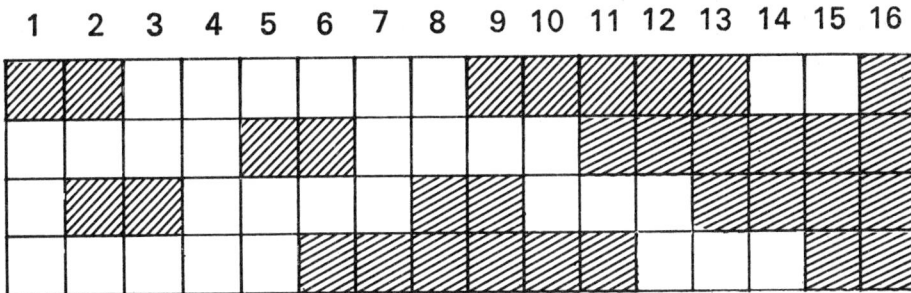

Performers play throughout each section. The conductor may vary the length of each section according to its effectiveness, or the duration of each section may be decided by the conductor in advance. Although it is desirable at this stage to emphasize one element at a time, the conductor will invariably have to refer to other aspects to make the exercise effective. For instance, injunctions to the brass to play loud for only very short periods of time in any section, and to the violins to use more bow occasionally, will be necessary to obtain any balance in sections designed to show the effect of tone-colour combinations in which they are involved.

The piece will be repeated following these or other suggestions which the conductor and players may have made. Perhaps this time the order of the sections may be altered.

Ex. 4

The above diagram should be all that is necessary to indicate the new order of the sections: 7, 6, 5, 4, 3, 14, 15, 8, 9, 16, 13, 2, 1, 12, 11, 10.

Yet again, variety may be asked for in each section, but this may be contradicted if some style of playing is so good that failure to repeat it would amount to a waste of an idea.

NOTE: Diagrams can be produced indicating other combinations:

Ex. 5

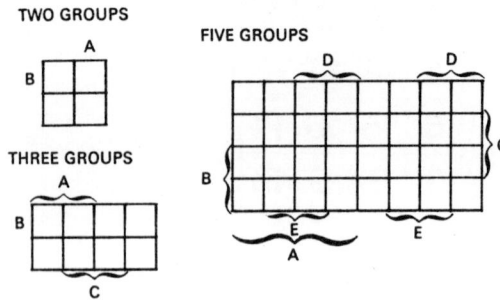

TWO GROUPS

THREE GROUPS

FIVE GROUPS

Volume

As volume was referred to in the last section, performers may decide that this is the next element to take as the basis for an exercise. (A teacher must be prepared to take suggestions from pupils rather than impose ideas that he has conceived before the session, but careful preparation and a thorough grasp of the problems involved will enhance the application of this principle and make it easier for the teacher to adapt and to channel pupils' ideas confidently and progressively.)

Where time permits a number of sections may be devised by the performers:

Ex. 6

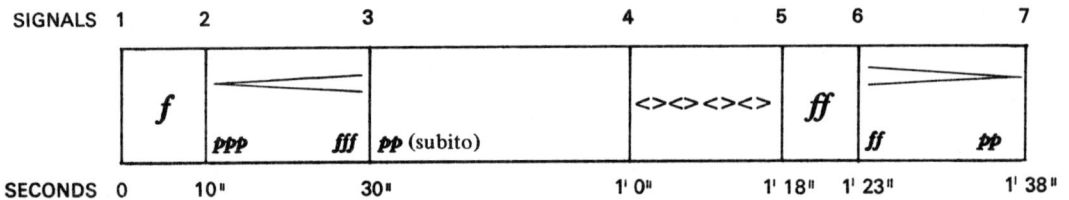

From 1 to 2 play *forte* (pitch, speed, etc., free)

From 2 to 3, one continuous *crescendo.*

From 4 to 5 four swells, individually timed by the performers.

Control is easy with the aid of a clock with a second-hand, but if manually conducted, 2–3, 4–5, and 6–7 will need a continuous movement (circular or vertical) in addition to attack and release signals, for the players must have a precise idea of the duration in order to control their increase and decrease of volume.

Much is to be gained by repeating this exercise several times. Volume is of the greatest significance in much modern music. Those whose experience has been confined to 'pop' or early classical music are not likely to project very large changes of volume without practice. In the exercise given, *mezzo forte* has deliberately been avoided as being an average volume with which players are only too familiar.

Intelligent use of a tape-recorder, once initial difficulties have been overcome, will enable the performers to become increasingly aware that volume may have some structural significance in music.

Even at this stage it is possible to make a composition by merely determining when each group of instruments is to play and at what volume. Such a digression is avoided here in order to give more detail, but what is done in a creative situation in the classroom is a matter for the teacher and pupils involved. Creative work cannot possibly flourish in the shadow of a scheme that all must follow in detail, and certainly no such scheme is being attempted here. The details described have occurred in various situations and it is possible to branch off at any stage.

Duration

Certain instruments make sounds which gradually die away (a suitable written sign for this is: ●⌒). The length of the sounds depends on size, resonators, etc. Ask all performers with such instruments to play a sound together and listen to their own sound until it has died away. Did all the sounds cease together? (It may be necessary to check that the performers are playing these instruments only.)

Now ask all performers to play a very short sound (● is a suitable sign). Some instruments will, of course, require to be damped by hand, and room reverberation and sympathetic vibration on instruments not in use may partly nullify the effect. For practical purposes wood-blocks, bottles, etc., give very short sounds only. That their sounds *do* gradually die away may be shown by recording the sounds, and playing them back at half or quarter speed.

Now ask voices, wind and strings to start together, making a sound lasting as long as possible. Naturally one expects the sounds to cease one after the other according to the breath or bow control and the nature of the instrument. All players should listen carefully as the total sound changes (a suitable sign would be: ●———————————).

Play and hear these three duration effects — short, dying away, and sustained — in some exercise such as the following. First the players make the sounds with the conductor's signals, and second, each player plays a new sound after breathing, or after the first has died away. Some discrimination regarding the density of *staccato* sounds may be achieved by asking for concentrated listening to the total sound:

Ex. 7

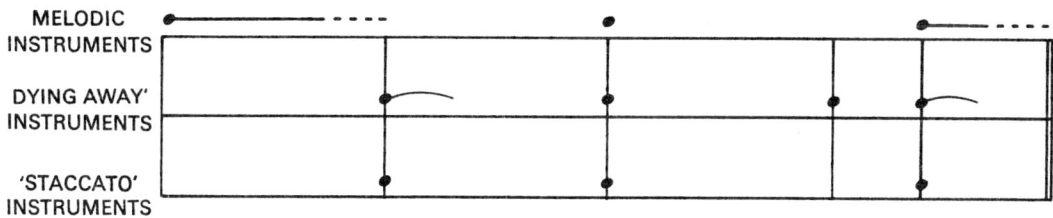

Exercises involving degrees of duration between the extremes of the longest and the shortest are suggested later in this chapter, under 'Texture', p.12.

Attack

Any variety that has been achieved in the work so far attempted will have resulted from the players' free improvisation with the elements of music that were not limited in any way. This variety should be encouraged, but specially attractive passages should be preserved and earmarked for expansion into compositions or improvisations of a special character. Attack will have been one of these elements, and as attack varies according to the nature of the instrument, some simple classification of instruments will be useful. Teachers should examine Example 8 and constantly fill gaps in their

Category	Capabilities	Electronic	Wind	Strings		Percussion				
				Bowed	Plucked	Metal	Wood	Glass	Skin	Miscellaneous
1	Indefinite pitch • ⋀⋀⋀ (1) (/\) (2)					Tin Cans Oil Drums	Wood-Blocks Claves Castanets Wood-Chimes		Small Drums Tambourines	Maracas Jingles Lagerphone
2	Definite pitch • ⋀⋀⋀ (/\)						Wood-Bars Xylophone	Bottles		Clay Plant Pots
3	Indefinite pitch • ⌒⋀⋀⋀ (/\)					Indian Cymbals Triangle Cymbal Nail-Chimes Gong Vibrators (3)			Bass Drum	
4	Definite pitch • ⌒⋀⋀⋀ (/\)				Piano Guitar Autoharp	Glockenspiel Metallophone Chime-Bars Tubular Bells	African Piano		Timpani	
5	Definite pitch • •—⋀⋀⋀ /\	Oscillator Organ	Voices Wood Wind Brass Accordion Harmonica Melodica	Violin Viola 'Cello Double-Bass				Wine Glasses		

(1) ⋀⋀⋀ tremolo
(2) /\ glissando
(3) Vibrators — Knives, steel rods, rulers, etc., plucked while supported firmly on table.

instrumental resources. Contact microphones may be effectively fixed to the sounding board or bridge of autoharps, 'cellos, and other stringed instruments, and also to gongs and cymbals. These may also be rubbed on a range of surfaces. Close positioning of microphones in general is also effective in bringing out sounds normally too weak to hear.

Many pieces written for schools are necessarily performable by different combinations of instruments, and consequently details of attack are to some extent left to the performer; unfortunately, the matter is often ignored and performances lack the subtlety which care and thought on the part of the teacher could have avoided.

Use of instruments

PERCUSSION

A wide range of beaters should be available for the percussion instruments: wood, with spherical ends of half-inch to two-inch diameter; rubber, including thin bunsen-burner tubing on the handle end; metal, including beaters of fine knitting-needle thickness; felt, of various degrees of hardness and thickness; cluster sticks, of wood, rubber and metal; wire brushes, double-bass bows, and the flesh and nails of the fingers. In general, the higher the pitch of an instrument the smaller and harder the beater. Lower-pitched instruments may be struck with a wide range of beaters.

Students should experiment with the full range of beaters and note the effect of striking at various points on the surface of the instrument, particularly for the larger instruments. No one beater should be regarded as the one normally used.

Some sort of tremolo effect ($\sim\!\!\diagup$) is possible on all instruments — by using two-beater strokes, rubbing, etc. *Glissando* $\diagup\diagdown$ is available on many instruments; on metallophones and xylophones interesting *glissandi* may be obtained by rearranging the bars.

It must be stressed that the best-quality instruments that can be afforded should be employed, and this applies to fruit cans and other sound-producing sources which were not made as musical instruments. Such things are unfortunately despised by many teachers of music, and except in infant schools, where a range of shakers and sand blocks is usually available, they are seldom to be found. The professional composer does not despise them. Britten uses crockery in *Noye's Fludde* (Boosey and Hawkes), but far more use could be made in the classroom of pieces where non-instruments are the sole or main sound-sources. In *Memories of You* (Universal Edition 14171), Cornelius Cardew suggests the use of glass ash-trays and a box of matches, such objects to be the only sound-sources of the piece. Christian Wolff's *Sticks* and *Stones*,* where the objects of the title make, or assist in making, all the sounds of the music, could well be used in the classroom. With verbal instructions only, they are excellent for bringing out creative abilities in those who possess little technical skill.

Example 9 lists the instruments to be used by the two percussionists in Berio's *Circles*. To obtain the instruments specified would be beyond the range of schools, but the teacher should purchase and make instruments to give a similar range of effects in his classroom percussion.

Various ways of using percussion instruments were discussed in *New Sounds in Class* (Universal Edition 14166) and the following possible ways of employing an

---

* Available from Experimental Music Catalogue, 26 Avondale Park Gardens, London W.1.

POSITION of INSTRUMENTS in the SCORE

3 wood blocks ① — also guiro
mexican bean ② — also wood chimes
log drum ③ — also sand block

marimbaphone ④

2 small bongos ⑤
2 large bongos ⑥ — also 1 tablas
3 tom tom ⑦

PERC. I

2 small timpani ⑧

3 triangles ⑨
hi hat ⑩ — also glass chimes
3 susp. cymbals ⑪ — the lower with „sizzles"
3 tam tam ⑫
5 cencerros ⑬
lu jon ⑭ — also celesta /sounds 1 oct. higher/
6 susp. chimes ⑮
/campane/

VOICE

(b♩) — approx. pitch /optional, exact pitch/ — spoken — on the breath — beats the tempo — gives attacks — clap

HARP

3 triangles ①
3 susp. cymbals ② — the medium with „sizzles"
1 tam tam ③
hi hat ④ — also glass chimes & clap cymbals

vibraphone ⑤ — also glockenspiel

PERC. II

4 chinese gongs ⑥
tamburo basco ⑦ — also 1 tablas
2 bongos ⑧ snare drum ⑨
3 tom tom ⑩ 2 congas ⑪
foot pedal bass drum ⑫
5 temple blocks ⑬
maracas ⑭ — also wood chimes /sounds 1 oct. higher/
xylophone ⑮

*sticks:
1. hard
2. soft
3. wood
4. metal
5. brushes

empty fruit-can as a sound-source are given as a further illustration of the range of effects available from very simple material:

Position: (*a*) held in hand.
(*b*) resting on soft surface.
(*c*) resting on table.
(*d*) gradually raised and lowered from a surface.

Striking points: (*a*) the covered end.
(*b*) rim of the covered end.
(*c*) the side of the can.

Beaters: (*a*) small wood, rubber or metal — held normally.
(*b*) point end of a knitting needle or pencil held vertically.

RECORDER

The following effects are possible in additon to conventional techniques:

(a) steady or *staccato* sound, with or without tongueing;

(b) wavy sound, by varying the wind-pressure;

(c) trills, and other finger tremolos, at various speeds;

(d) flutter-tongue;

(e) fingerings to produce more than one sound;

(f) noisy fingering without blowing into the instrument;

(g) *glissando*, by sliding fingers over holes;

(h) blowing, or singing with fipple covered;

(i) singing while fingering the same pitch, including *glissando*;

(j) singing and playing in counterpoint;

(k) covering and uncovering the fipple while blowing and fingering with the left hand;

(l) removing the lower joints and obtaining *glissando* effects by sliding the flat hand across the end of the joint.

PIANO

Methods of attack may be varied to include:

(a) Playing on the keys: (with or without the sustaining pedal) single sounds, chords (possibly clusters with flat hands and/or forearms), rolled chords, trills, tremolos, sounds of various lengths, overlapping sounds.

(b) Playing on the keys with the sustaining pedal depressed and damping the strings of the keys played after the attack or with the attack.

(c) Harmonics: depressing some keys silently, inducing sympathetic vibrations in the strings by playing other keys (see Example 10).

(d) Playing on the strings (with and without sustaining pedal): plucking with finger or nail at various points on the strings, striking the strings with various beaters, sweeping the strings with hands, brushes, etc.

(e) In *Amores* and *Sonatas and Interludes* (Peters), John Cage fixed screws, bolts, pieces of rubber, and so on, to the strings and produced from the piano the sound of a new percussion orchestra. This can be done most easily and with greater possibilities on a grand piano.

STRINGS

Schaeffer's *String Trio* is a catalogue of effects. Penderecki's *Threnody: To the Victims of Hiroshima* and *String Quartet* employ the following special effects: highest note (indefinite pitch), playing between the bridge and tailpiece, playing on the bridge and on the tailpiece ('cellos and double-basses), striking the belly of the instrument, striking the strings with the hand, and tremolos and vibratos of different speeds.

Group work

Ask the group to experiment with their instruments. Observe and listen carefully. Ask individuals who have produced unusual effects to demonstrate them to the remainder of the group and encourage each performer to list the various ways of playing his instrument.

In Figure 2 each of the four teams played in eight of the sixteen squares. Have the groups separate and ask each group to decide on a common procedure: a different one for each of the eight small squares. Ask them to mark these in some form of notation on their copies, in any common order.

After each group has played its eight sections separately, they should play in combination. The conductor should listen intently, allowing the sections to be fairly long and assisting with gestures and words where appropriate. Much help will be needed in determining balance and speed of playing. Performers should be urged to listen to one another, and individual help may be offered where necessary.

Offer and invite comment after recording and playing back. Repeat the process.

Location

Where absolute precision in pitch and rhythm are required performers are placed closely together. With freer rhythmic relationships between the parts many positions in space become not only possible, but also an integral part of the performance, or of the composition. Instruments and players should not be regarded as immovable in the classroom; various layouts should be tried and pieces built on the layout structure. Some use of the normal layout of tables in rows is made by Brian Dennis in *Experimental Music in Schools* (Oxford University Press, 1970). The primary-school group layout of tables is suited to a mobile structure. My own *Music for 30 Percussion Players* (Universal Edition 12951) was written after seats had been re-arranged in a semicircle. Britten's church operas contain examples of sounds moving, as do numerous other works, and the possibilities of music and movement deserve further exploration in schools. The article by Henry Brant, 'Space as an essential aspect of Musical Composition', in *Contemporary Composers on Contemporary Music* (Holt, Rinehart and Winston, New York, 1967), covers thoroughly certain aspects of the subject.

For our present purpose we can demonstrate the effect of location as follows:

(*a*) Pointing to players at random, far apart, front and rear, in order along the rows, separately, together, and in the reverse direction. Players may operate successively in concentric circles from the outer to the inner and vice versa, clockwise and anti-clockwise, one circle playing continuously against successive individuals in other circles, and so on.

(*b*) The conductor's arm moves horizontally from left to right, or right to left; players start when the hand points to them the first time and stop when pointed to a second time. Make up schemes that omit some tone-colours and limit ways of playing, and so on.

(*c*) Divide the group into four sub-groups according to their position in the room and irrespective of instrument. Perform a square piece with this arrangement (the sub-groups will need to discuss and rehearse separately).

Pitch

Consideration of this important parameter has been delayed until now partly to demonstrate the importance of other elements of music and the ease with which they may be employed in the classroom without notation, or with very simple graphic notation, and partly to give all a chance of performing irrespective of technique. It should be borne in mind that in modern music all notes of the chromatic scale are of equal importance. The widest possible variety of sound should also be admitted from those instruments which emit no clearly defined pitch and those which produce defined degrees of pitch that are not contained within the equal-tempered chromatic scale (for instance, most plant-pots).

More than any other parameter, pitch is related to the structure of the instrument and the technique of the player. A note is immediately available on any keyboard or fretted instrument, but not on most wind instruments or members of the string family without preliminary technical accomplishment. Therefore, with a desire to involve all technical abilities and a wide range of resources, pitch cannot initially play the part that one would normally expect without limiting the sound to such a point as to withdraw most of the excitement necessary to interest the majority, even though a certain knowledge of pitch will of course have been gained from traditional musical work.

Many successful pieces have been written without pitch specifications (there are numerous examples in the *Experimental Music Catalogue* and in the *Music for Young Players* series published by Universal Edition). The use of register is perhaps the simplest and most effective way to begin to get away from chaos in pitch.

TOTAL RANGE OF A FAMILY OF INSTRUMENTS

This is often overlooked, particularly with pitched percussion instruments, because of the frequent employment of octave transposition and the common disregard of the octave in traditional work involving tunes and accompaniments. The following ranges of typical classroom instruments may be found useful:

Ex. 11

WRITTEN

Bass Metallophone or Xylophone | Alto Metallophone or Xylophone | Soprano Metallophone or Xylophone | Chime-bars | Glockenspiel

SOUNDING

The bass, alto and soprano metallophones taken together have a compass of over three octaves. They may be regarded as one instrument split into three overlapping registers, giving seven possibilities of registration: bass, alto, soprano, bass + alto, bass + soprano, alto + soprano, and bass + alto + soprano. Instruments should be given frequent silences, but two instruments should often be employed together in the overlapping part of their compasses. Morton Feldman's *In Search of an Orchestration* (Universal Edition 15324) uses pitch mostly from this standpoint.

REGISTERS OF INDIVIDUAL INSTRUMENTS

The usual method is to divide the effective compass for an individual player into three approximately equal areas — high, middle, and low. There are many examples of Feldman's work in graphic notation where only register is used for pitch definition. *The King of Denmark* (Peters), for solo percussionist, is a graph score to be played softly throughout, the instrumentation being mostly at the discretion of the performer. Each box is equal to MM 66—92. The piece begins in box 1 with seven high sounds, followed by a short high sound in box 4, a long high sound in boxes 8—11, and so on. R indicates a roll:

Ex. 12 MORTON FELDMAN *The King of Denmark*

7		♪			1 --- ---			1 ------- ♪	1↑				♪	R	7
									5		♪	♪	2		5
									R -----		♪	♪			2

Copyright © 1965 by C. F. Peters Corporation, 373 Park Avenue South, New York, N.Y. 10016
Reprint permission granted by the publisher.

The division of pitch into registers initially enables at least some of the players of instruments of indefinite pitch to take part, with three wood-blocks, three plant-pots, and so on, and where there is a shortage of instruments, chime-bars may be distributed in threes — high, middle, and low.

Consider now a simple square piece (Figure 2) based on pitch. Each of the four sub-groups will need eight possibilities; though only seven are available if we consider register only — high, middle, low, high + middle, high + low, middle + low, and high + middle + low.

The group will think of other limitations; for example, players who have a number of pitches available in each register may limit themselves to the use at times of one sound, two sounds, etc.; those players who have a number of notes in common may limit themselves to the use of one or more specific sounds. The effectiveness of the combined effort will depend on volume, duration, and other elements.

Texture

A texture results from the combined effect of the elements already considered — tone-colour, volume, duration, attack, location, and pitch. Our pieces up to now have usually shown control in only one of these elements. It becomes increasingly obvious that by deliberately considering a number of these elements and by combining and juxtaposing the resulting textures, it is possible for a wider range of people of all ages to compose music than was hitherto feasible. The possibilities are limitless, and individual compositions attain character by the limits that are imposed and the elements considered. Webern defines in detail all elements except that of location; Bach normally leaves volume, speed, and attack to the discretion of the performers, and in the *Art of Fugue* instrumentation is not defined; Feldman, in *The King of Denmark* quoted above, limits the percussionist to the use of fingers, hands and arms. The composer may give the score exactly, as in Boulez's *Le Marteau sans Maître* (Universal Edition 12652), or the performers may be given some choice, as in Stockhausen's *Stimmung* (Universal Edition 14805). At school and college level, the use of material which gives some degree of choice makes possible the employment of resources and skills available and gives useful musical training to the participants, but the value of fully notated pieces, which have their own value in developing precision and technique, should not be overlooked or underestimated.

The distribution of different types of attack has a great effect on texture:

PERIODIC ATTACK
(*a*) Regular attacks of one or more beats.
(*b*) Regular rhythmic patterns (*ostinati*).
(*c*) Irregular patterns.
(*d*) Combinations of these with a common beat or with different beats for groups or individuals.

APERIODIC ATTACK
This will not have been studied in traditional work but will be found essential; it may sometimes be used in conjunction with periodic work. There are numerous possibilities, but the following may be useful to begin with:
(*a*) Sounds made on given signals from a conductor or group-leader (free timing, without beat structure, signals being given at the psychological right moment).
(*b*) Sounds on, immediately before, or immediately after signals from a conductor or group-leader, the time of the attack being varied by the players within these limits (used in Cardew's *Material* – Universal Edition 14171).
(*c*) A small group of sounds – *allegro, moderato, accelerando, ritardando* – beginning or ending on a signal from the conductor or group-leader.
(*d*) A continuous sound, possibly tremolo, beginning and ending on signals.
(*e*) Playing at various speeds according to signals or at the individual player's discretion, or by timing with a stop-watch or clock that has a large second-hand. In the first example the density of sounds is only partly controlled:

Ex. 13

SIGNALS	1		2		3		4		5		6
		FAST		SLOW		MEDIUM		ACCEL.		RIT.	
CLOCK TIME	0"		5"		15"		20"		30"		45"

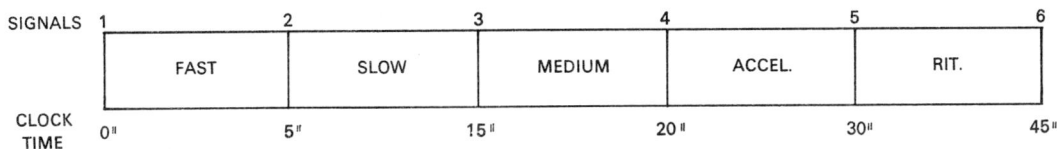

(The timing of the signals 5 and 6 in this example needs to be known by the players, possibly indicated by a circular motion of the conductor's hand.) The density in the above example will depend on the number of performers and on their individual interpreations of the signs. The next example gives complete control over the density of sound; the signals will have to be periodic to preserve this control:

Ex. 14

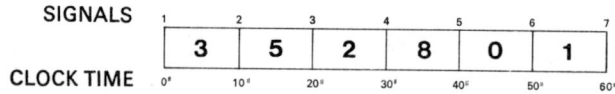

SIGNALS

1	2	3	4	5	6	7
3	5	2	8	0	1	

CLOCK TIME   0ˢ   10ˢ   20ˢ   30ˢ   40ˢ   50ˢ   60ˢ

Example 15 illustrates a possible interpretation of box 2 by seven players.

Ex. 15

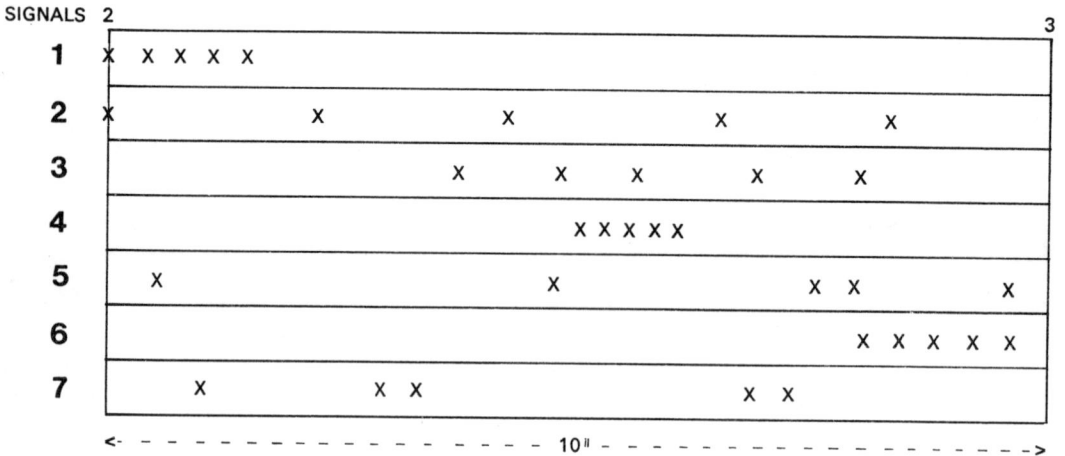

Possibly a preliminary piece would be useful in which each box was of the same duration and contained the same number of attacks. Various interpretations would be possible — varying the timing of attacks in each box; retaining the timing offered in box 1 until a signal is given to make a change, either by the conductor or by group-leaders independently; each player retaining his timing for box 1, and changing his timing when he feels it to be desirable; some players retaining an unvaried interpretation, others freely varying the timing, with possible interchange of these different functions; each player developing the pattern he makes in box 1 (for instance, player one in Example 15 could develop as in Example 16):

Ex. 16

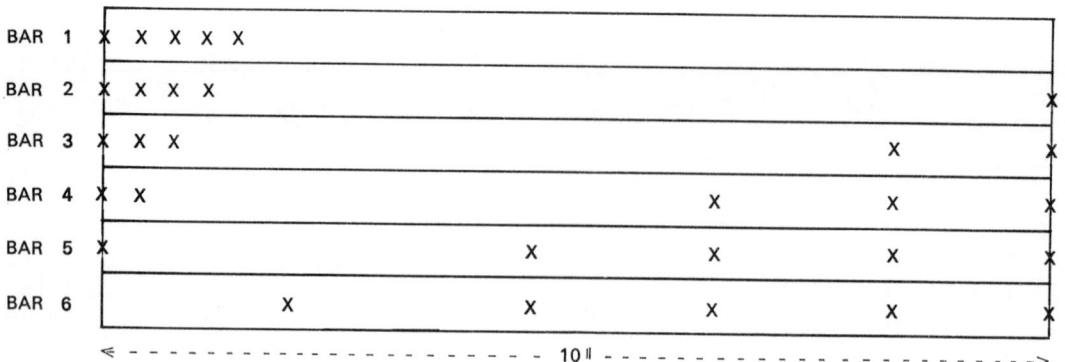

14

It is important to record and play back tape-recordings of these pieces and exercises. The good performer always hears what he is doing within the general context. Particularly in a large body of players, every performer has a different position and therefore a different aural point of view, and it cannot be assumed that any one performer has the same aural experience as the conductor, or hears exactly live what is heard from the tape amplifier. By careful listening, performers may become aware of sounds which were not heard on the recording, thus storing in their memories experience for their own compositions.

In Example 14, control was only imposed on the density of the attacks; a development of this exercise shows further differentiation, durations having been defined. The three parts are numbered according to the categories of instruments given in Example 8.

Ex. 17

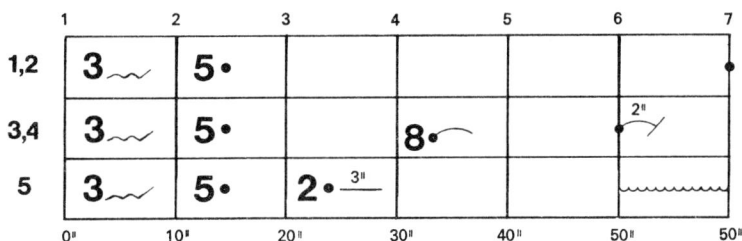

After signal 1 — three short tremolos (say, each less than one second).
After signal 2 — five *staccato* sounds.
After signal 3 — two sounds (for each of the relevant players, each sound lasting three seconds).
After signal 4 — eight sounds which are undamped.
After signal 5 — no attacks, but some sounds may still be dying away from the previous section.
At signal 6 — a continuous tremolo until seven, together with sounds manually damped after two seconds.
At signal 7 — a *staccato* attack coinciding with the end of the tremolo.

The next example is a further elaboration of the previous one. Some indication of volume is given, and registers are indicated for pitched instruments (for example, at signal 4, five high, two middle and one low sound, permutated in any possible way):

Ex. 18

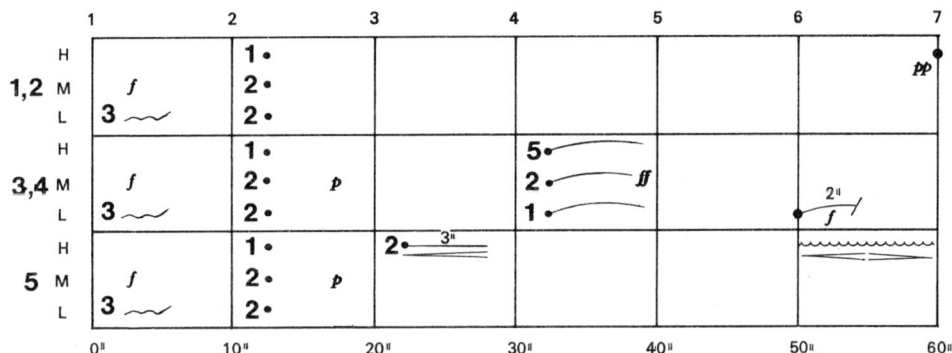

15

No deliberate attempt has been made in this exercise to contrast different types of instruments in density, nor, except at 6, in the manner of playing. Also, some instruments or groups of instruments could have been omitted.

Further experience may be enjoyed by again dividing the group into four sub-groups – encourage them to discuss, rehearse and notate, in some simple manner, eight contrasted textures. The groups may play their textures separately and then in all the combinations of a 'square' piece. Suggest modifications for making this more effective; perform and rehearse the modifications, record, and so on.

From these beginnings one hopes that students will continue to explore sound for themselves, and compose for themselves and their friends. Thousands of people who have finished their formal education find enjoyment and renewal in painting and other visual arts; perhaps others will find equal value in music – as a composing art as well as a performing one.

The music made until now has been stimulated by interest in the sound-sources themselves. A topic such as the beginning of Genesis will give further inspiration and understanding of composing problems. We suggest a piece associated with all or some of the following successive sections:

Chaos, Darkness and Light, Land and Sea, Sun, Moon, and Stars, Animal Life, Man.

The topic may be considered only from the musical point of view, or perhaps in conjunction with art, religion or other subjects.

Various methods may be adopted:

(a) Sub-groups may separately make and perform music for the whole sequence.

(b) Each sub-group may take a single section and perform in turn. It would be possible for the sub-groups to alternate the functions of music and dance.

(c) Each group may be made responsible for notating a sketch of part of the music for the whole group to perform.

(Younger performers are more likely than others to remember what they have invented, and no notation whatever may be necessary. Alternatively, the 'notation' may take the form of free art-work that has an independent, artistic value of its own.)

Whichever method of the three is chosen, the following will have to be considered:

(a) Which of the sections are to be used (other ideas or modifications may be suggested)?

(b) The instrumentation for each section – especially if the students have had little experience of making their own music. Different instruments for each section will ensure great contrast; if the same instrument is used in two sections, particularly adjacent ones, ask for some indication as to the actual function of the instruments in each section to ensure contrast (high/low, periodic/aperiodic, fast/slow, etc.). Lack of contrast is only really acceptable if it is quite deliberate. Do not overlook the voice – performers on any instrument may be asked to sing when not employed with their instruments.

(c) Having decided on the basic use of the resources, discuss the length of the whole piece and the length of the sections. Normally, the interest will be increased with sections of uneven length, and presumably those suggesting lengths will have in mind what they feel is possible with the resources available. The lengths suggested will probably have to be modified as the piece develops; less effective sections may have to be shortened and experiential time may not relate to the clock-time suggested. Consideration of clock-time may eventually be abandoned, but its early use can help unification.

(*d*) In the working-out of individual sections, does one section overlap with another? Does a section consist of one texture, or are there several successive or overlapping ones? What are their relative lengths?

(*e*) Complete and partially complete sections should be discussed, modified, and at each stage, compared with the initial sketch so that relationships to the whole are always in mind. Minimum information should be clearly written in a code understood by everyone (signs will proliferate because suggestion will often be more individual and complex than the notation used in this chapter is capable of expressing).

A product of uneven quality will almost certainly result from the limited time that is likely to be available, but so long as the leader has shown enthusiasm and discrimination, the participants will derive some pleasure from it. If they have become aware of new possibilities, conscious of some of the difficulties, and believe that if there were more time many improvements could be made, composing has become a part of their being, and repeated encouragement in future sessions should increase their confidence.

2. Transcription

Issue each student with a sheet of paper. Ask them to fold their paper in half and carefully crease it down the centre, and then tear the paper along the fold.

Have the group been aware of the sounds that were made? Three distinct sounds of folding, creasing and tearing? Or were they expecting to write, and more concerned about finding their pens?

Inform the group that the pieces are to be used as musical instruments (as with all instruments, use the best quality available). One piece of the paper is put away for future use; with the other piece the group experiment and produce as many different sounds as possible.

After some practice ask individuals to play, each to make a different sort of sound until the ideas of the group have been exhausted. After each idea has been demonstrated ask the group to perform it together; here questions of volume, timing, and speed will have to be considered. For example:

1. Tugging
(*a*) All together on the first beat of a 4/4 bar.
(*b*) In four groups, each on a different beat of the bar.
(*c*) *Accelerando, ritardando.*
(*d*) In four independent groups, each timed by a leader.
(*e*) All independently, avoiding any general impression of beats.

2. Tearing
(*a*) Very slowly, making a continuous, quiet sound.
(*b*) All together, *accelerando.*
(*c*) In continuous succession, *accelerando* (timed by tearing when pointed at by the conductor, whose arm moves in a continuous lateral sweep).
(*d*) In 3/4, with a short tear on each beat.

Such effects as tapping with the fingers, shaking, blowing across the edge, blowing across the end of rolled paper, flicking with the fingers, crumpling, and so on, could also be considered in similar detail.

Try out one idea in different ways, simultaneously and in succession; try out a number of different ideas simultaneously. Make a short piece with suggestions from the group – point out that the music need not be consistently in a fixed number of parts.

Divide the students into groups and ask each to make its own paper piece. Have each group play its piece before the other groups.

Select one of the paper sounds used by a group; ask all to take an instrument, so that there is a good variety in the group (the voice may of course be used). Ask each performer to find on his instrument the nearest equivalent to the paper sound. Have each performer play his transcription separately. Sounds will be produced in unusual and interesting ways, and players of similar instruments may come forward with quite diverse effects.

Ask the performers to transcribe other paper sounds, making sure that the contrasts on the instruments are as strong as the contrasts in the paper effects.

Now send the groups away again to transcribe their own paper pieces for their instruments (players of similar instruments may have to agree on the transcription effect to be used).

Some of the transcriptions will be more adventurous than others, but the exercise should have had some success in focusing the attention of the group on the subtlety of attack. It is significant that small groups, who have been sent away to make up short pieces without any reminder of the subtle effects they obtained in transcription, may return with pieces where there is no interest in the attacks used. For instance, the effect which a performer may have invented as the equivalent of tugging on a metallophone – two rubber beaters striking the instrument a minor third apart without being allowed to rebound – is completely forgotten, and a return made to *laissez vibrer* pentatonic broken chords. This is not evidence of the uselessness of the transcription described, but evidence that much more work along these lines is needed, especially if the training in creative work has not been started at a young age. The paper-piece transcription is a start, and should be supplemented by:

(*a*) Instrumental pieces transcribed for voices.

(*b*) Vocal pieces transcribed for instruments.

(*c*) Music for a small group transcribed for a larger one.

In addition to the value of transcription as an experience in its own right, the process can also serve as a useful medium for involving students more closely with modern techniques of composition. Development along these lines is introduced in Chapter 7.

3. The voice

A great deal can be done without the use of manufactured instruments at all. Rulers, paper, pencils and bits and pieces from a junk-yard can provide a wide variety of sound, as can the human body by clapping with cupped or flat hands, striking the fingers of one hand with those of the other, rubbing the hands, stamping feet, slapping knees, flicking the fingers, and so on. Above all, we have the infinite variety of resources offered by the human voice. Although song is basic to any scheme of musical education, the voice as a sound-medium often remains relatively unexplored and is quite indispensable in textural and other work along modern lines.

Example 1 is a very primitive piece that serves to illustrate the four basic kinds of sound obtainable from the voice. The performers may select their own texts independently, or invent sentences and sounds as they go along:

Ex. 1

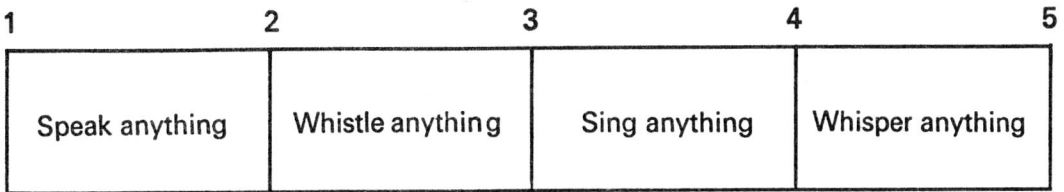

These contrasts of sound are very telling, and immediately suggest further differentiation. Before this is followed up, however, the piece will probably have to be repeated because of difficulty experienced with whispering (some will confuse this with quiet speaking. Encourage everyone to whisper loudly, in a *stage* whisper, to demonstrate the difference.) Perhaps all did not change at the signals, nor stop precisely at 5. Establish clearly that performers are free to do as they wish, *within defined limits.*

Whistling
This is taken first as it has only one quality (without the use of fingers). This beautiful sound is underrated and some find it difficult, but it is well worth cultivating. Although it is possible to articulate with the clarity of bowing (with and without tonguing), such sophistication has been avoided in Example 2, so as to throw the emphasis on relative pitch:

Ex. 2

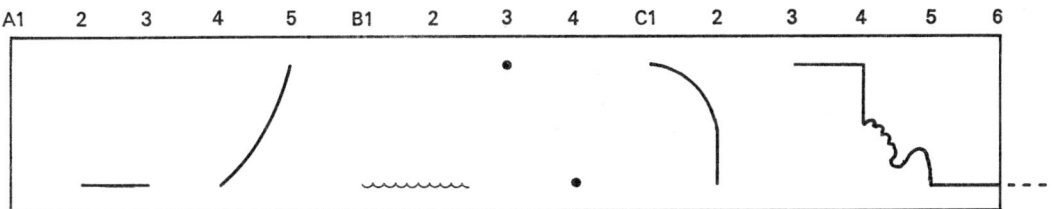

No exact pitch is indicated, only shape and register, so that with several performers we have, at each attack, a chord or cluster.

The signals are numbered and lettered, as in a number of Brian Dennis's instrumental examples in *Experimental Music in Schools* (Oxford University Press). As Dennis says, this makes it easier for performers to keep their place in the score. Signals with two hands at A1, B1, etc., give them added confidence.

At signal A1 – a high staccato sound.

At signal A2 – each performer selects a low sound and holds this until signal 3; if this is not possible, each performer breathes as necessary, retaking the same note again.

Signals A4 to A5 – this sound could last at least ten seconds; shapes such as this could be indicated graphically by the conductor.

Signals B1 to B2 – trill of a tone or a semitone.

At signal C5 hold a low sound, breathing as necessary. Take no breaths after C6 but hold the sound as long as possible (i.e. performers end one after the other).

Ex. 3

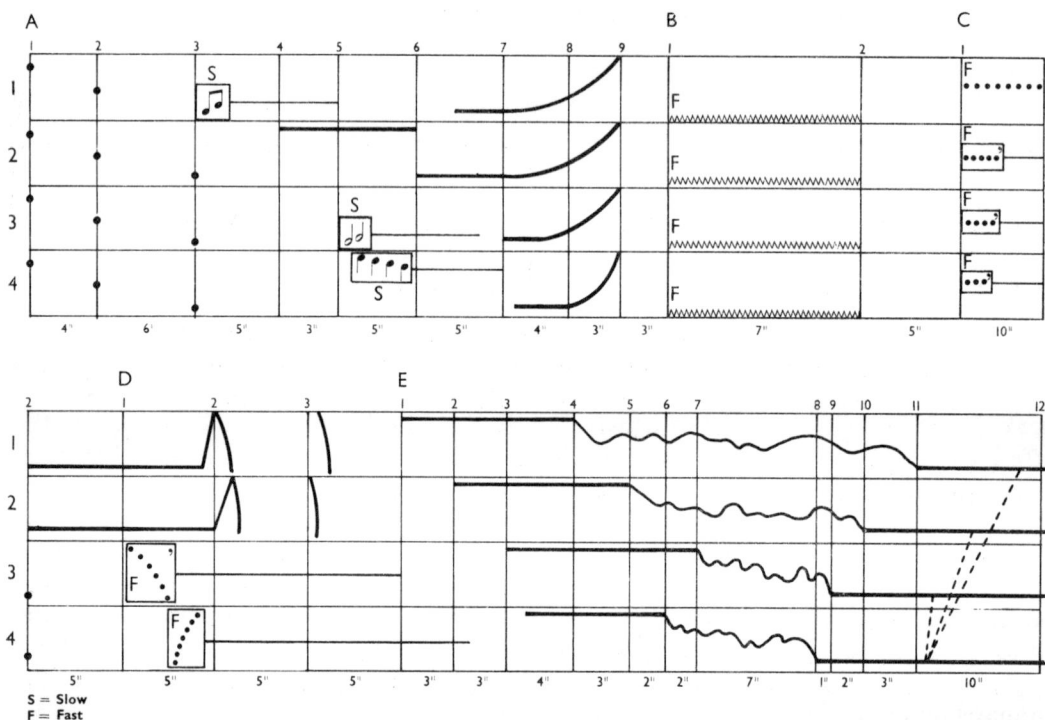

S = Slow
F = Fast

Example 3 is a development of Example 2. The continuity in the graph should be evident in the sound, and to achieve this, players breathe to suit themselves but not at a signal where a change of texture is involved in their own part (e.g. in all parts at C2). A suggested clock-time is given below each frame.

Part 1: A3–A5 – a continuous slow low trill (mm ♩ = 60), independently timed by the performers.

Part 3: ·A5 until after A6 – again mm ♩ = 60, therefore a slower trill than in part 1.

Part 4: After A5–A7 – crochets at a similar speed in a repeated, step-wise, descending pattern – stop at A7 whether the pattern has been completed or not.

Part 1: C1 — continuous, rapid, repeated *staccato* sounds.

Part 2: C1 — rapid groups of five *staccato* sounds, with a short pause after each group, until C2.

Part 3: D1 — rapid, descending *staccato* sounds until E2, with a short pause after each descent.

Part 4: D1 — rapid ascending groups of *staccato* sounds without pauses, each performer beginning at any time after D1 and ending at any time after E2. At E11 *all* hold a low sound, making a glissando, one after the other, to the sound of a selected performer in group four. The unison so obtained is held, with breath as necessary, until E12. Each performer then holds the sound as long as possible without further breath.

Whispering, speaking and **singing** may now be further differentiated. With each performer using his own text, or all using a common text independently, we may:

1. vary the speed of the performance of the text(s), to slow, medium, fast, *accel., rit.*, possibly with pauses between words or phrases;
2. vary the volume;
3. vary the pitch.

Example 4 may be tried with whispering, speaking, singing, or a mixture of these with texts as suggested. (Whispering is an effective texture but can be tiring if kept up for too long.) Perform the texts for the duration of the given lines. Invent other pieces using texts in similar ways.

Ex. 4

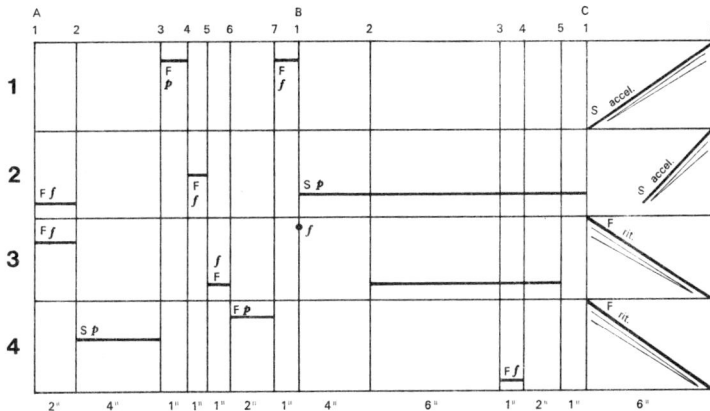

Texts may be further differentiated:

(*a*) There might be a common text throughout — performed at independent speeds or in a common metric or speech rhythm.

(*b*) There might be one text for each part.

(*c*) There might be a different language for each part.

(*d*) A different style could be used for each part. (Cage's *Aria*, 1958, published by Peters, consists of a coloured graph with vocal sounds and words from a number of languages. The singer must allot to each colour a style of singing — coloratura, jazz, nasal, etc.).

(*e*) Parts could use words and phrases associated with a particular scene — a factory, the seaside, the home (in the latter case a separate style might be set apart for television).

Each idea suggests differences in form. The last proposal would suggest a free construction. Possibilities include: (i) the use of random numbers to give times when individuals or groups would start to whisper, speak, or sing phrases given to them or invented by them; (ii) the allotting of a certain number of phrases to be uttered within given time-limits; (iii) a planned 'mobile' of monologues, dialogues, etc. Then (i), (ii) or (iii) might also be used as a background to some other event (improvised melody, a speech, a poem, etc.).

Texts may be specially selected for alliteration and onomatopoeia (Roget's *Thesaurus* is particularly useful here). Bernard Rands, in *Sound Patterns 1* (Universal Edition 14647), makes excellent use of unvoiced consonants in group whispering effects ('she sells sea shells', etc.).

Examples 3 and 4 could be performed using voice sounds instead of texts. A list of the more important of these is now given:

VOWELS

These may be used over a range of duration and pitch — in whispering, speaking and singing.

Long vowels	AH	AI	EE	AW	OH	OO
As in	PA,	MAY	WE	ALL	GO	TOO?
Short vowels	a	e	i	o	uh	u
As in	THAT	PEN	IS	NOT	MUCH	GOOD

VOICED CONSONANTS

These may be used over a range of duration and pitch in whispering, speaking and singing. The quality of most of them may be altered by forming the mouth for various vowels.

L as in LONG   TH as in THEY
M as in MEN   V as in VERY
N as in NOW   Z as in ZEBRA
NG as in SING   ZH as in PLEASURE
R (rolled) as in RUN

UNVOICED CONSONANTS

These may be used over a range of duration and pitch in whispering. The pitch is indefinite and may vary continuously (*glissando*) by altering the vowel formation of the mouth; for example:

Ex. 5

S (u) _ _ _ _ _ S (uh) _ _ _ _ S (i) _ _ _ _ _ _ _ _ _ _ _ _ _

S as in SUGAR   F as in FRED
SH as in SHERRY   TH as in THICK
CH as in CHANGE   H as in HOAX
J as in JUDGE

HARD CONSONANTS

These are *staccato* explosions only.

B as in BED	D as in DAD
P as in PAT	K as in KEY
T as in TEAM	G as in GORE

To these may be added sounds such as the click of the tongue (variable according to the vowel formation of the mouth: 'click', 'cleck', 'clack', 'clock', 'cluhck', 'cloock'. Syllables formed from vowels (diphthongs, triphthongs) or vowels and consonants will also prove useful. Apart from the normal vibrato at various speeds, the sound may be modified by patting the mouth while singing (as used in Bernard Rands's *Sound Patterns 1*, Universal Edition, 1973), or using cupped hands over the mouth for muting and vibrato. Nasal singing will produce another quality, as will singing into a kazoo.

The examples which follow illustrate some contemporary uses of the voice by composers that could be useful models for educational work. Example 6 shows the use of voiced *glissandi* (S.1 and T.1), unvoiced *glissandi* (S.2–7 and T.2–4) and a spoken

Ex. 6 TADEUSZ BAIRD   *Etiuda,* for vocal orchestra, percussion and piano (1961)

PWM-4729

rolled 'r'. The cluster chords in the Altos and Basses (each singer holding a different given pitch within the given ranges) involve eight different vowels, with humming and whistling, to give a 'neutral' background to the other moving parts. The instrumental parts, not given in the quotation, consist of rapid finger-patterns on untuned timpani (a similar texture to the rolled 'r'), and a gong tremolo, starting at the centre with a *glissando* to the edge, which complements the moving voice-parts. The *glissandi* serve to differentiate the various voice-sounds. (In educational work the clusters of exact pitches would probably be replaced by the use of register — 'sing any sound in the middle range'.)

Ex. 7

Example 7 is part of the fifth section of the same work, and shows rhythmic ostinato use of consonants, in combination with the tapping of the fingers of one hand with those of the other, and clapping. The quotation is a part of 'A', in an additive form, which is a useful scheme for educational purposes. In this case there are five parts: A, A + B, A + B + C, A + B + C + D, A + B + C + D + E. B, C, and D are similar rhythmic shapes for timpani, piano, and percussion respectively, E being sung-vowel *glissandi* by solo voices.

Ex. 8   KRZYSZTOF PENDERECKI   *St Luke Passion* (1965)

Example 8 shows a *staccato*, jazz-like humming effect, in spacing notation, with an indeterminate pitch-shape indicated. This is accompanied by double-bass *pizzicato* and timpani *glissandi*.

In the same score, Penderecki shows gradual changes of vowel-sound from humming:

Ex. 9

27

Ex. 10

A development from the sharing of a row of notes between a number of parts is shown in Example 10, where the syllables of the words 'popule meus' are divided between the voice parts. Detailed perusal of the whole score of this work will be rewarded by the discovery of a wealth of ideas that may be adapted for use in educational music. In *Two Poems* for chorus (Universal Edition 14705), David Bedford makes use of the same device. He also employs some voices on the vowel-sounds only

Ex. 11   DAVID BEDFORD   *Two Poems*

of words that are complete in other voices (Example 11). The avoidance of a regular beat effect by the use of duration sequences on different time-scales would be replaced by spacing, or other notation, in educational music; the use of note sequences (here taken from the whole-tone scales) would however be feasible.

Christopher Small's *Black Cat* (Universal Edition 14659) is a good example of a short piece for schools consisting of descriptive spoken words with instrumental effects. A further development of this would be the writing of words over the instrumental parts in such a way that the speaker (or singer) becomes the conductor. This has been effectively done with choral speaking (Example 12).

As well as the Christopher Small piece and the *Sound Patterns* series of Bernard Rands, useful items in the *Experimental Music Catalogue* include *Phonetic Music* by Hugh Shrapnel, *Voice Piece* by Christopher Hobbs, *Mass Medium* by Bryn Harris, and other pieces. *When Words Sing* by R. Murray Schafer (Universal Edition) will give courage and inspiration to many.

Much of the best educational music is of course written for or by a group of people with specific abilities and is therefore rarely published. Example 12 is the beginning of a work for a comprehensive-school choir and orchestra; the carefully contrasted vocal effects in Example 14 begin a piece by a student for fellow students to sing. This educational work is most satisfying when it leads to spontaneous group composition and improvisation within a community.

Example 15 shows a scheme which makes use of a plainsong melody in various ways and offers opportunities for various degrees of improvisation. Soloists at A3 may use either or both of the words 'Kyrie eleison'. The improvised solos here may possibly be derived from the plainsong, perhaps by the omission of some sounds:

Ex. 13

KY - - RI - E E - LE - I - SON

At A4 each singer or group is allotted one note of the melody. The diagram illustrates the cluster-like structure, with swellings marked where a sound would normally be repeated. The imitations at B3 need not be exact; some distortion is expected, depending on memory and improvising skill; there would be no limit as to key — if there is one at all. Singers choose either or both of the words 'Christe eleison' for imitation. The improvisation should be repeated as necessary, stopping at B4 irrespective of the point reached in the phrase. The chorus continues with the material started at C1, and each singer completes a phrase before changing to the new material when signal C2 is given. After the conclusion of the solo which starts at C4, the soloist hums any one sound until after C5, with breath as necessary.

Instruments may be added with supporting or contrasting textures, and sections could be interpolated for instruments alone.

Ex. 12

	'TWAS	BRIL –	LIG	AND	THE	SLI –	THY	TOVES
Recorders								
Oboe								
Clarinet								
Bassoon	LOW 𝆑 p							
Trumpet	Mute on						con sord.	MED. sf p
Trombone	Mute on				LOW con sord. mf	gliss.		
Percussion I	Chime-Bars	struck f						
Percussion II								
Violin	Mute on							
'Cello	Mute on				LOW con sord. mf	gliss.		

	DID	GYRE	AND	GIM –	BLE	IN	THE	WABE :
Recorders	HIGH f	LOW						
Oboe		HIGH f	LOW					
Clarinet			HIGH f	LOW				
Bassoon				MED. f	LOW			
Trumpet		sf p		sf p				
Trombone								
Percussion I								
Percussion II							GONG (Tea-Tray)	
Violin							con sord.	HIGH p LOW
'Cello								HIGH p LOW

30

Ex. 14

S — *pp* Moderato / AH

A — *p* / SH ... Whisper / ka. T. B. D. / **Fast** / *mf*

T — Whisper / ka. T.B.D. / **Fast** / *mf* ... *p* ee ... *pp*

B — *p* / BRR ... BRR / *mf* ... SS / *p* ... (i) / SH

1 2 3 4 5 6 7 8 9 10 11 12 13

Ex. 15

A1 — ♩ = 120 approx. / (and/or 8ve lower) KY - RI - E - E - - - - - LE - I - SON

A2

A3 — Chorus members in succession / many short, syllabic solos by different performers, ♪=120± / sometimes overlapping, sometimes separate / KYRIE/ELEISON/KYRIE/ELEISON

Slow wavy sound, *senza tempo*, when not acting as soloist

A4 — Slower / KY - RI - E - E ... LE - I - SON

B1

B2 — Soloist I / melismatic improvisation, free, extended / CHRISTE ELE-ISON

B3 — Chorus / simultaneous imitations of material from B2 on any vowel sounds

B4

B5 — Soloists I & II / melismatic improvisation / I as at B2 / II new material / CHRISTE ELE-ISON

B6 — as at B3, but imitate soloist II

B7

B8

C1 — Soloist II / same material, or variation of previous solo / CHRISTE ELE-ISON

C2

C3

C4 — Soloist I / Very slow, syllabic / mm / KYRIE ELEISON

C5

Chorus — start on the sound A; immediately the soloist ends, continue with melody A1, but each singer at his own speed; repeat the melody a number of times, each time higher (high voices) or lower (low voices). Lengthen a different note of the melody each time. / KYRIE ELEISON

Chorus — sing the shape of A1, widening the interval to extend over the full compass of the voice - quick, irregular speed, *staccato f* / KYRIE ELEISON

Chorus — continue, but gradually omit sounds from the shape till 3, 4, or 5 remain / *Rit.* / *p subito*

31

4. Music and art

A musical view of five pictures

PICTURE ONE

Six students arrive for a two-hour session of creative music-making. The students are rotating on a three-session scheme between art, music and movement; this group did art in their first session, and as Elisabeth McClosky's picture (see back cover) seems full of ideas which could be paralleled in music, we decide to make a piece related to it.

There are basically three areas in the picture:

(a) The outer area, composed of thick vertical strokes in blue, with hints of purple, white, and black.

(b) A fine irregular texture of brown, with hints of other colours. Superimposed on this are four white speckled areas and a bold flat-white circle.

(c) A blue-black area, the texture being rather a distorted version of area (a), the blue, however, being brighter. Superimposed are rounded black areas relating to the white areas in (b).

The group is asked to experiment with the sound resources in the room and then discuss the choice of tone-colours that will represent the various areas in the picture.

The following decisions are made:

(a) Metallophones and glockenspiels;

(b) Maracas, cymbals, pins in tins, sleigh bells;

(c) Two pianos, played on the strings only, with pedal.

The lecturer suggests that it might be wise at this stage to decide on the overall form of the piece. Should we 'read' the picture from left to right, arriving at the following structure?:

$$(a) \dotfill$$
$$(b) \dotfill$$
$$(c) \dotfill$$

The group are unanimous that this is not the procedure they want. They see more musical parallel in working from the outside of the picture towards the centre. The lecturer then draws the following layout:

$$(a) \dotfill (b) \dotfill (c) \dotfill$$

The group considers this, and decides after some discussion that this should be modified to become:

$$(a) \dotfill (b) \dotfill (c) \dotfill (b^2) \dotfill$$

with some difference in (b) on its second appearance.

From the initial stimulus of the picture the group now thinks more and more exclusively in musical terms.

In view of the small number in the group, and their limited technique (there are no music students), all are to be employed in each section to obtain the most interesting effect. Because of the variety of resources employed there will be difficulties in

33

obtaining continuity when performers change to different instruments at the changes of section. The piece is therefore recorded in separate sections; a stereo tape-recorder is used with separate recordings on channels 1 and 2, the whole being played back in the mono mode (an equivalent result could have been obtained by superimposing).

Section (a). The group experiments on metallophones and glockenspiels with various beaters, especially on the metallophones. These experiments are closely observed by the lecturer, who draws the attention of the group to the most interesting features of individual performers, and these are tried out in turn by the whole group. There is general agreement that the use of wide cluster-sticks, with which an octave or more of notes (black and white) may be sounded together, will produce a rich resonance that seems appropriate to the colour and texture of this section of the picture. The performers play in this way perhaps a little too busily. The lecturer suggests that before striking their instruments again performers should listen to the general resonance. This slows down the intervals of attack, there is no metrical co-ordination, and performers play quite independently.

Section (b). Maracas, tins, sleigh-bells and tambourine are laid on a large table. The section is performed reasonably well, each performer taking up different instruments for short periods. The main defect is the noise made as instruments are laid down again. A repeat performance shows a great improvement in this, but to avoid accidents during the recording, thin sheets of foam plastic are laid on the table. The section is tried many times, each repeat being preceded by suggestions for improvement by the group (for example, as the tambourine often swamps the more delicate sounds, the players suggest that it should be played more softly and with longer silences; maracas may be played singly, both together, in short shakes or swirls, and producing single *staccato* sounds; also, of course, there is *silence*).

Silence is most important. Not only is the texture varied when an individual performer stops playing, but if the individual concerned listens during that silence, he is automatically training himself to listen while performing. This is bound to bring about a consequent improvement in the general ensemble.

The white areas of section (*b*) are to be represented by cymbals. The group decides that there shall not be too many cymbal sounds (there is no mention of making the number of cymbal sounds equal the number of white areas), and that a leader shall deliberate when and how the group plays. Thus, a sound from the leader which is allowed to ring on is rapidly followed by a similar attack from each of the other performers. This method seems to give a musical effect comparable to the visual effect of the slightly irregular white patches. The more regular white circle is represented by a concerted, *staccato* attack.

Section (c). Here there is no need for repeated criticism and rehearsal, for by good fortune, an excellent effect is hit upon immediately. Both pianos are used with pedals depressed throughout; the strings being gently swept with the hands on piano one, and melodic shapes extending over the whole range of the instrument are plucked on piano two. The black patches of the picture are represented by a few strokes on drums with hard, felt sticks.

Section (b2). The tambourine and maracas are omitted, the sleigh-bells and tins retained. In addition, six single sleigh-bells, of different sizes and pitches, are used detached from their holders. Much practice is needed to obtain a texture of the desired thickness. Towards the end the single sleigh-bells play alone, with a gradual thinning of the texture.

In this last section it is finally decided to discard the cymbals and substitute some Elizabeth Shaw Mint Crisp Tubes. (These are soft plastic cylindrical containers with hard plastic lids. By squeezing the tube the lid flies off and a popping sound is heard. A variety of popping pitches is obtained by cutting the tube to different lengths.)

Before recording, the relevant lengths of the sections are discussed. The final plan with the recording scheme emerges as follows:

Ex. 1

SECONDS	0		30	45		90	120		180

CHANNEL I   [Texture (a)]   [Cym.]   [Texture (c)]   [Pop]

CHANNEL II   [Texture (b)]   [Texture (b2)]

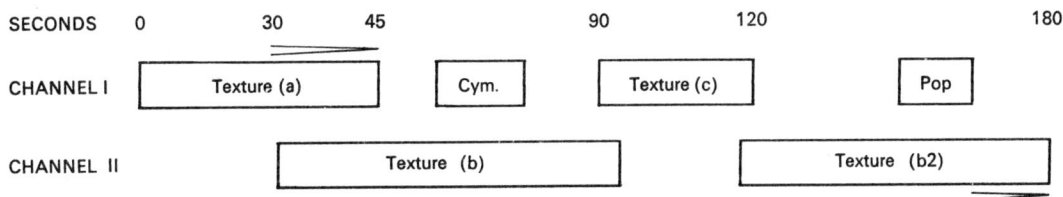

The group listens to the performance of its own composition and is quite elated by the result. Faults in recording technique have left short silences between sections (b) and (c) and between sections (c) and (b2). After some indecision the group decides that these silences should remain.

The group has enjoyed the session; next week they will go to a movement session, taking with them their paintings and their tape-recording. With only one session of music in the creative arts course, wide resources were used to demonstrate their necessity in the classroom. Care was taken, however, to limit the number of textures used, but if the course were of longer duration, such large resources would not be used in a three-minute piece.

PICTURE TWO

This student picture (see back cover) was painted in red and green, the paint being applied to the paper directly with the hand. Twelve students were asked to select an instrument for an improvisation to be related to the picture, with the limitation that the sound from the instrument was to be made by striking or rubbing the sound-source with the hand. No sounds were to be made by shaking or blowing, nor by using beaters or bows. Many soft and delicate sounds on almost all percussion instruments were effective with the fingers, and louder sounds, involving higher harmonic content, with the finger-nails. Recorders were effective in quiet passages (sound of tapping fingers hard on the holes only).

The various elements of the painting were discussed:

(a) The horizontal finger-strokes across the middle of the picture, starting as a very dense mass at the extreme left of the picture and gradually thinning to become a complete hand-impression on the right.

(b) The hand shapes pointing upwards and downwards from this centre line.

(c) The oblong shapes in two colours.

Improvisation 1. All performers interpreted any or all elements as a pointer was moved slowly below the picture from left to right.

Improvisation 2. Performers selected any one of the elements to interpret.

Improvisation 3. The elements selected for interpretation were decided by the group as a whole. This was found to give the most satisfactory result.

Only a short time was spent on this work, but some development of musical sensitivity resulted from it. (It was only later discovered that the picture should have been rotated through 90 degrees anti-clockwise to become a Christmas tree!)

PICTURE THREE

This picture (see back cover) was quickly interpreted in a very simple way. Each performer chose his sound-source and everyone performed throughout the piece. The picture was considered as a twelve-bar structure in 4/4 with everyone performing in crotchets. It was divided as follows:

Ex. 2

^{1}a	^{2}b	^{3}a	^{4}b
^{5}b	^{6}a	^{7}b	^{8}a
^{9}a^1	^{10}b^1	^{11}a^2	^{12}c

The letter a represents the colour green, with a^1 and a^2 as different shades of a; b represents red, with b^1 as a different shade; c represents black. The contrasts required in the first nine squares varied from player to player, but most of them made the contrasts by change of pitch, change of pitch-register, or by change of attack. Square number 12 involved a number of changes, particularly in volume. The effect was very satisfactory, especially when balance between the instruments was obtained.

Our improvisation was rather ragged because the players lacked experience and had so much to think of at once. More practice would of course result in greater precision, but some slight raggedness suits this particular picture, in which the squares are not geometrically accurate. Had the performers developed greater precision, the initial spontaneous, ragged effect could have been recaptured by asking them sometimes to play deliberately just before the beat or occasionally after the beat.

Many other interpretations are of course possible. A longer version could be made, of 48 bars, with each of the small squares equal to one beat. Here, the variety of orders in which the squares may be taken is much increased. Again, tone-colours could be aligned to different colours in the picture. Alternatively, a number of players could interpret the picture, maintaining a common beat but with each player taking squares in an independent order. This procedure may result in cross-rhythms; for example a player may decide to start with the outer small squares, beginning in the top-left corner and moving clockwise, giving:

Ex. 3

$$\frac{4}{4} \quad a \mid b \mid a \quad \frac{7}{4} \quad b \quad \frac{4}{4} \quad a \quad \frac{7}{4} \quad c, \text{ etc.,}$$

The pale red background of the picture could be considered as a constant element (for instance a random chord, vocalized) that is held, without variation, throughout the performance of the detached sounds. The 'square' piece introduced in Chapter 1 could be used in conjunction with the picture, involving silence and consequently greater variety:

Ex. 4

a	b	a	b
b	a	b	a
a¹	b¹	a²	c

The interpretation of the first of three performers could be:

Ex. 5

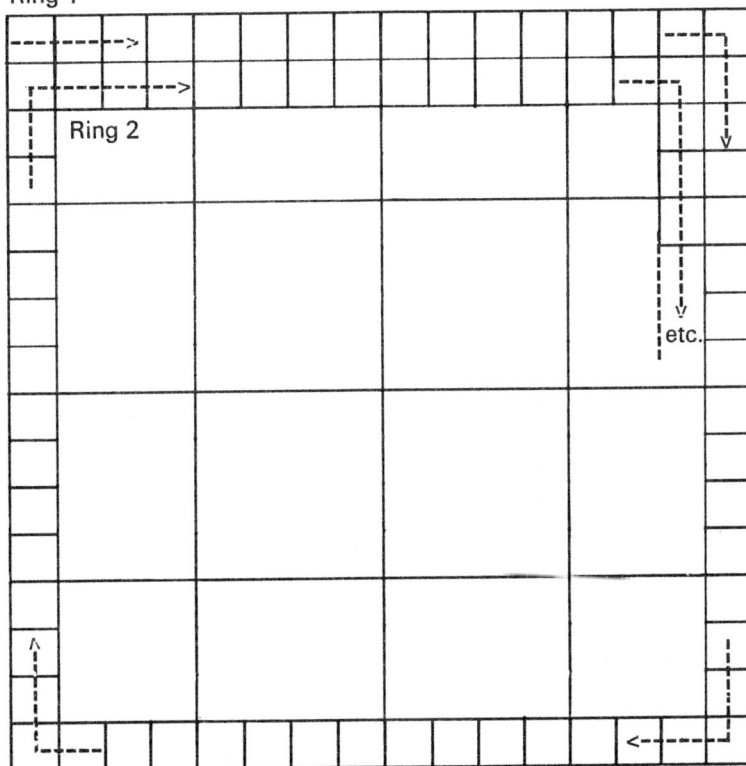

The second and third players could interpret in the same way with different pitches. The notes used by the three performers for *b* could be recorded on a tape loop, and then played throughout the performance at a lower volume than the live sound but always audible in the rests. Each player could perform the eight rings of small squares in turn, beginning in different corners and in different rings (see Example 6).

Ex. 6

A written-out version of a part of this would be:

Ex. 7

PICTURE FOUR

This picture (see back cover) is full of delicate colour and rapid whirling movement. It seems to suggest, in music, exotic tone-colour and continuously moving sound with occasional sustained sounds; nothing in the nature of *staccato* or *legato* melodic movement appears to be implied. The *glissandi* should be varied in speed. This can be effectively achieved on melodic percussion instruments by dragging a beater in a circular pattern, varying the size and position of the circular movements.

PICTURE FIVE

This long picture (see cover design – original size 28'6" by 2'6½"), was specially made by Mary Davies for musical interpretation. White, black, and varying shades of brown and yellow are used. The picture is in three overlapping sections: bottom right – curved and ragged shapes; bottom left – curved shapes of varying degrees of intricacy, and on the top large regular shapes, mostly rectangular. Newsprint is a uniting feature of the texture.

The art students who performed instinctively chose sound-sources and used them for their colouristic effects rather than for producing melodic shapes. They also displayed considerable ability for using the instruments dramatically, forcibly, and well contrasted in the different sections. An amplified, mistuned autoharp with the strings plucked, struck and scraped at varying volumes was effective, together with piano, plastic lids, stones, and so on. In the first improvisations the performers were co-ordinated by a very slow-moving pointer. It was decided to interpret the irregular shapes freely, but the small intricate curved patterns demanded regularity of beat (not necessarily a common one), and repetition. Specific shapes were allotted to individuals to interpret as they wished in the section on the top.

Later, work was carried out without a co-ordinating pointer: firstly, with free interpretation of everything by all; secondly, a free interpretation that included repetition of features which specially appealed to individual performers; thirdly, by allotting different sections to individuals to be performed concurrently.

There was never need to come to common agreement on the musical meaning of, say, black, which was variously and simultaneously interpreted by different performers as a low chord, a very loud sound, a *crescendo*, and so on.

The changing shapes and the reaction of one player to another sometimes resulted in an individual deliberately changing his meaning at the recurrence of a colour.

AN AUDIO-VISUAL EVENT

To involve large numbers of students in art, music, movement, and lighting, a structure planned to last about one hour was devised as follows:

Ex. 8

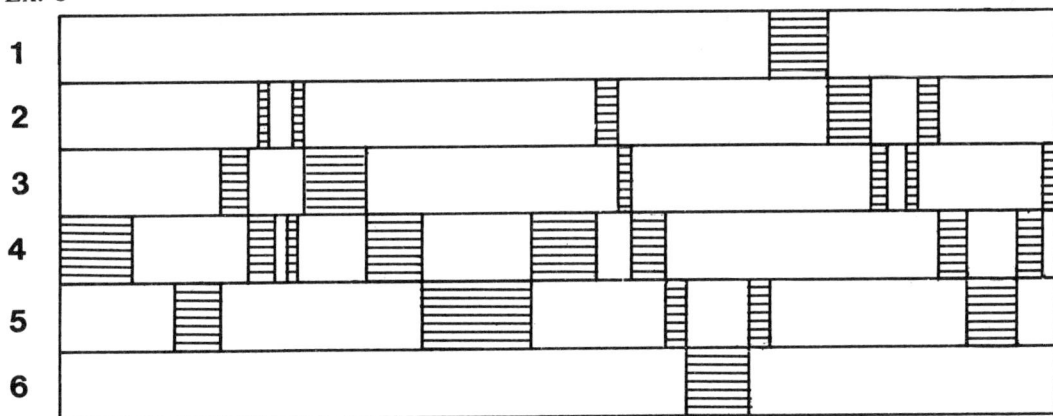

This was drawn on six scales, these being allotted as follows:
1. Tape and amplification.
2. Tuned percussion, including piano.
3. Untuned percussion.
4. Transistor radios, short-wave radio and pop record.
5. Woodwind and strings.
6. Various visual events.

The musicians were timed by a large illuminated clock with second and minute hands; lighting technicians co-ordinated watches with this. Other visual events were timed from lighting.

The six horizontal divisions in Example 8 above, signify variously tape and amplification: in the case of tape, playback of material taken from a recording of an instrumental rehearsal at different speeds, from different channels; in the case of amplification, channel 1 or channel 2, reverberation, and ring modulators.

In the instrumental parts the horizontal divisions indicate the superimposition of six chords and also the distribution of material between the performers.

For the visual, see Example 9.

1. *Lighting.* Interesting display may be arranged for its own sake.
2. *Dance.* A central area was reserved for dancing. Spotlights were focused on the dancing area at the allotted times, but this did not preclude extending the dance outside these time-limits.
3. *Audio-visual collage.* A large display board was erected visible to the audience. Glass and plastic bottles, straw mats, corrugated paper, metal tubing, lids, etc., were fixed to the board to make an interesting visual display, and to make interesting sounds when rubbed with small crystal microphones. The aural effect was only moderately satisfactory for it was soon discovered that considerable practice was really necessary to acquire the technique needed to produce to order the interesting range of effects of which the objects were capable. Great control over the pressure, angle, and speed of movement of the microphones is needed. The amplification was

turned on and off in time with the appearance and fading of light.

4. *Mobiles.* These were made from aluminium strips and were suspended from six random points above the dancing area. They were lowered and lit at appropriate times and in various combinations. Glockenspiels played various textures only when mobiles were lowered. The mobiles were agitated by tugs on the ropes when music or other events demanded it.

Ex. 9

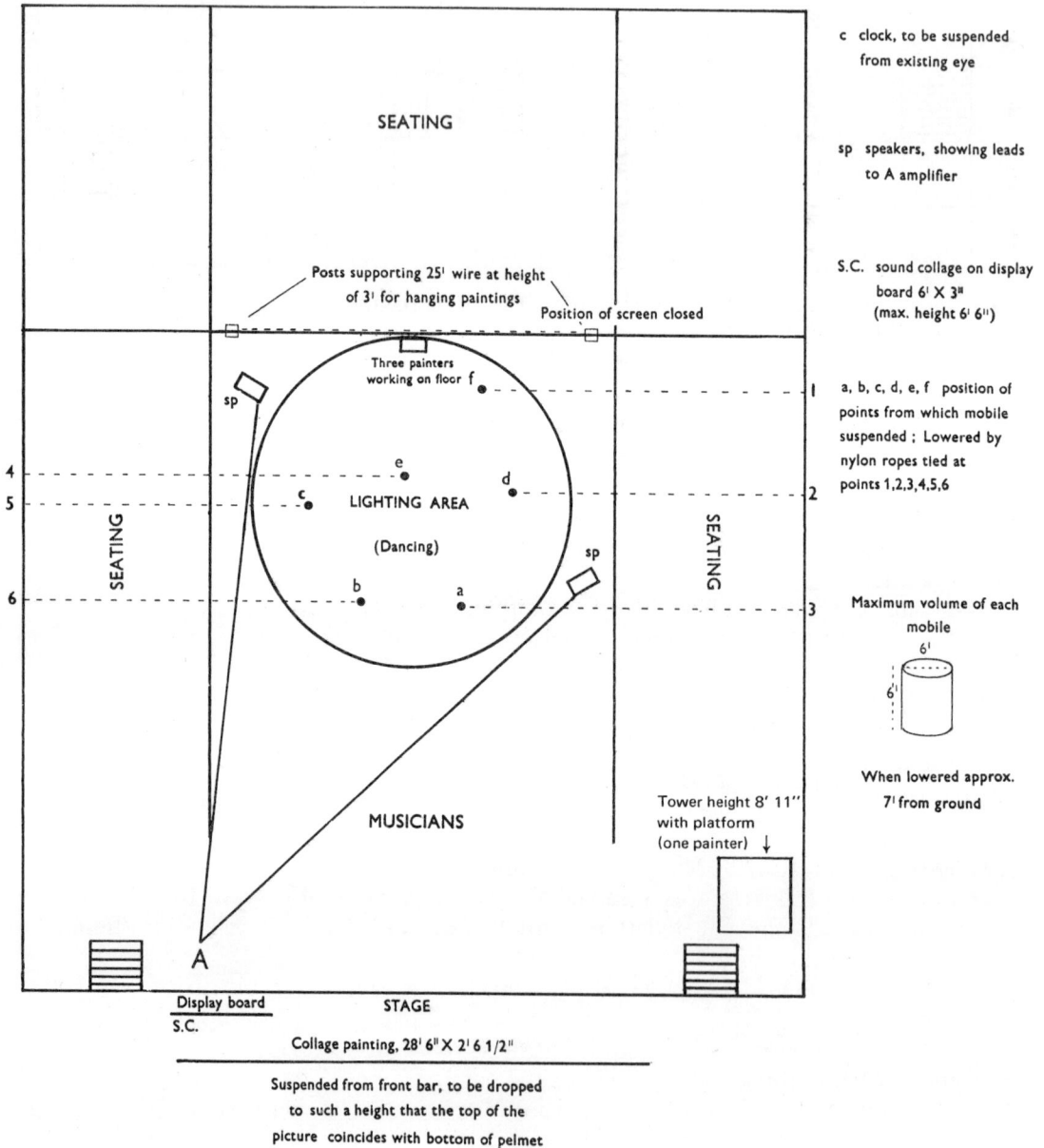

c   clock, to be suspended
from existing eye

sp   speakers, showing leads
to A amplifier

S.C.   sound collage on display
board 6' X 3"
(max. height 6' 6")

a, b, c, d, e, f   position of
points from which mobile
suspended ; Lowered by
nylon ropes tied at
points 1,2,3,4,5,6

Maximum volume of each
mobile

When lowered approx.
7' from ground

SEATING

Posts supporting 25' wire at height
of 3' for hanging paintings

Position of screen closed

Three painters
working on floor f

sp

LIGHTING AREA

(Dancing)

sp

SEATING

SEATING

MUSICIANS

Tower height 8' 11"
with platform
(one painter)

A

Display board
S.C.

STAGE

Collage painting, 28' 6" X 2' 6 1/2"

Suspended from front bar, to be dropped
to such a height that the top of the
picture coincides with bottom of pelmet

0 1' 2' 3'

40

5. Music and movement

This might take the form of an experimental period with, say, twelve students. Divided into two groups, they are all involved at some time in both playing and dancing.

Section One
Initially, those in group 'A' perform as dancers and those in group 'B' are instrumentalists.
Six sets of three chime-bars, chosen at random from a chromatic range, are arranged on the floor in the form of a large circle:

Ex. 1

Members of group 'B' sit at the chime-bars and improvise. A simple pattern is asked for, and it is suggested that the chime-bars are played in the following rhythm, in the order left, middle, right; right, middle, left:

It is then agreed that the first section shall be performed as illustrated in Example 2.
The pattern is cumulative, each player starting when the previous player has played the pattern once. After the sixth player has played the pattern once, the dancers (group 'A') begin in the same order and at the same time-distance of one pattern, making free, flowing movements around their partners in group 'B'. The playing and movement continues until player 'B1' judges that the section should draw to a close.

---

*This section is the outcome of a session in collaboration with Gill Macey.

Ex. 2

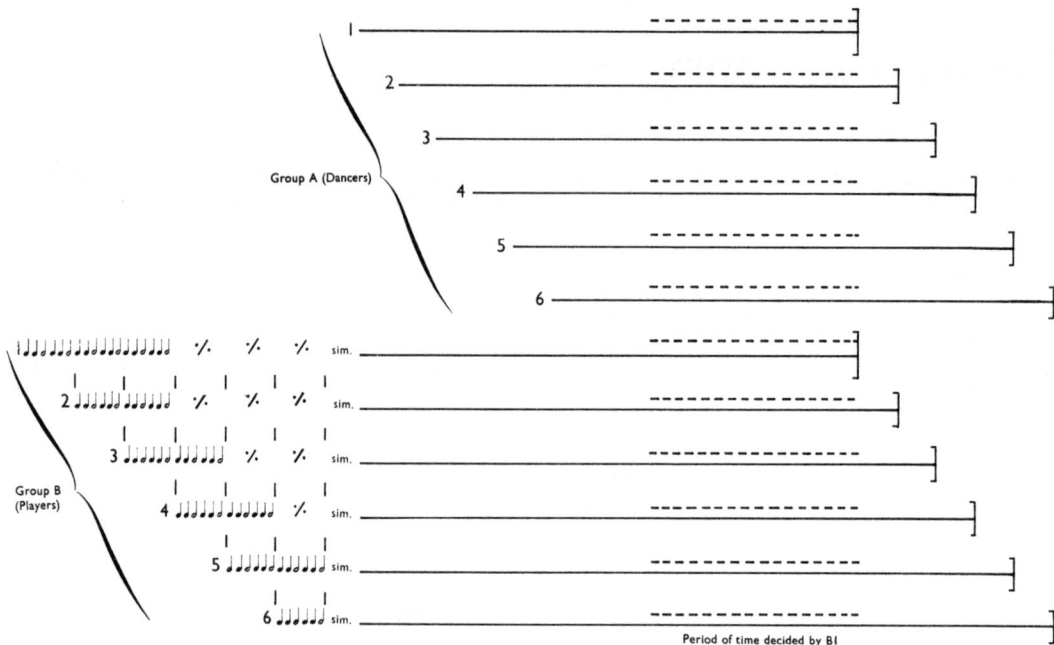

The players then stop in the order in which they started, and the dancers sit as their partners cease playing. There is now silence and stillness.

After some discussion, it is decided that one player shall have an old aluminium frying-pan (struck with a rubber beater and sounding rather like a gong). On the first stroke, all dancers move to the centre of the circle and remain in a pose, with arms upraised, until the second stroke of the pan. At this point, chime-bars are rapidly rubbed across with the beaters to produce a tremolo effect; there is a slow *diminuendo* from very loud, and the players cease when they can no longer hear sounds from their own instruments. The dancers move with gradually decreasing excitement, and end once more by sitting near their partners.

Section Two
Various possibilities that could constitute the basis of a second section are discussed. Should the chime-bars be played in different ways, with or without movement? Should movement without playing be considered?

The performers finally decide that this new section requires instruments not yet used. A random selection of three wood-bars (see *New Sounds in Class*) is placed beside each set of chime-bars (with wood beaters). Players and dancers exchange functions; group 'A' will play and group 'B' will dance. The members of group 'A' experiment with the instruments, but interesting and simple ideas do not readily emerge; perhaps they have not yet recovered from their dancing exertions! Eventually it is decided that there will be a number of sub-sections, each started by a sound from the pan, and with the player of the pan judging the effective lengths. For each sub-section, all players play in their own time according to the following instructions:
(*a*) fast playing on the left wood-bar only;

(*b*) playing at a medium speed on the middle wood-bar;

(*c*) very slow playing on the right wood-bar;

(*d*) fast drag of the beater across the three bars from left to right, with fairly long time-intervals between successive drags;

(*e*) rapid improvisation on all three bars.

Again, a dance is improvised, this time with the dancers moving anti-clockwise around the circle. If the movements are not in keeping with the dry, *staccato* sounds (so different from the chime-bar sound, with rubber beater, *laissez vibrer*), ask the dancers to stop and listen to the contrast between slow chords on wood-bars and on chime-bars.

Sections one and two are now put together. The students have been working for an hour and need a rest; they are asked to return in half an hour with suggestions for the next section.

Section Three

In sections one and two, the dancing has been improvised to the music. In section three, the initial decision is that all shall dance in well-spread groups of four, each group having a different percussion instrument: group 1 – maracas, group 2 – tambourine, group 3 – sleigh-bells, and group 4 – a small drum. The groups are quite independent of one another in rhythm and style, so the general effect is that of a dancing–musical mobile. One member of each group sets up a style of playing and dancing, to which others of the group react in dance. When this player judges that the dance should end, he (or she) stops, and with the other members of the group, freezes in a pose (a pause of at least ten seconds is suggested). The same player judges the effective time for the group to restart, and passes the instrument to another performer in the group, after which the process is repeated. Each player sets his or her own different style, and care must be taken to ensure that the pauses for all groups do not coincide exactly. The section ends when each performer has played the group instrument and all are in a statuesque position.

Section Four

It is important that the work is completed within the 1½ hours allotted, as it is unlikely that these performers will ever have a second session together. Having agreed that only two more sections can therefore be added, it is left to the lecturer to offer suggestions that will allow the time remaining to be fully utilized for practical work.

The four instruments used in section three are distributed and placed with the chime-bars and wood-bars. Each performer is to dance with a chime-bar in one hand and a beater in the other. There are three sub-sections, the beginning of each to be indicated by the playing of repeated notes by a selected performer:

(*a*) Each performer strikes his or her chime-bar, holds it close to the ear, and moves freely; stopping when the sound ceases. The effect of moving sounds is most exciting. The process is repeated many times – the strikes are of course not in time with others, for the sound-duration varies with the size of the bar.

(*b*) With the performers stationary, chime-bars are struck and moved in the air in wide sweeps – up and down to the floor and at other angles. The process is repeated when the sound disappears, over and over again.

(*c*) Sub-sections (*a*) and (*b*) are combined to form an exciting mixture.

Section Five

For this, the last section, the performers are seated in six pairs, as at the beginning of the work; there is no dancing this time, and the instruments are shared. Again, there are three sub-sections, and each is heralded by a stroke on the pan:

(*a*) Free improvisation on all instruments.

(*b*) Free improvisation — chime-bars and wood-bars only.

(*c*) Free improvisation on wood-bars only, quite softly, the players stopping in any order.

Finally, all five sections are put together. Many hours might be spent in developing the subtlety of both the dancing and the playing; some sections could be expanded to advantage and others added (for instance, a series of duels could be devised in which performers strike the chime-bars of other performers). But the procedure outlined above was actually carried out with a group of students. No score was used, all the movement and music being memorized.

6. Music and numbers

Once a sense of beat is established it is possible to develop a working knowledge of multiples and fractions of the beat. The following approach should be a useful supplement to that normally adopted. Although the examples given here are written out, most of them are intended to be used without the aid of notation. Where notation is used in connection with practical work, the form adopted in Example 1 has the advantage of providing a single sign for 'do something' and another for 'do nothing'. (*a*) could be used initially as an accompaniment to (*b*), etc., but may soon be discarded for a visual beat only. Two or more patterns may then be combined. If these are thought of in terms of a common measure, as in the 4/4 of Example 2, performers will each need a written part or a score. The parts will be easier to play, with or without a score, if the example is rethought as in Example 3, the attack for each player being on 'one' and the conductor giving unaccented beats.

Ex. 1

(a) [musical notation]

(b) [musical notation]
1 2 | 1 2 | 1 2 |

(c) [musical notation]
1 2 3 | 1 2 3 |

(g) [musical notation]
1 2 3 4 5 6 7 | 1 2 3 4 5 6 7
etc.

Ex. 2

A [musical notation]

B 4/4 [musical notation] etc.

C [musical notation]

([musical notation])

Ex. 3

A 3/4 [musical notation]

B 4/4 [musical notation] etc.

C 5/4 [musical notation]

Ex. 4

As the number of such concurrent patterns increases the texture will benefit from contrasts of tone-colour. The sounds need not all be short, and the complexity and interest may be heightened by superimposing another pattern (for instance of pitch and attack, as in Example 4, where a pattern of three is superimposed on each part of Example 3). Such procedures may be readily devised by the groups themselves. The texture of Example 4 repeats every sixty beats, and perhaps parts, or time patterns only, could be interchanged at this time-interval (A to B, B to C, C to A); at the same time, the beat speed could be altered.

A freer texture can now be made with the groups or individuals selecting and changing patterns as desired, with periods of silence after one or more such changes.

Ex. 5

A number series, such as that in Example 5, may now be used as a pattern. This pattern repeats every twenty-eight beats, and after working in unison, a group of twenty-eight players could enter in canon at one-beat intervals. After this the 1, 2, 3, 4, 5, 6, 7 series could be used by some groups against the 7, 6, 5, 4, 3, 2, 1 series in others. Alternatively, the two could be combined into 1, 2, 3, 4, 5, 6, 7, 6, 5, 4, 3, 2, 1 and used canonically, or different parts of the series could be performed concurrently:

Part A	1, 2, 3, 4, 5, 6, 7
Part B	1, 2, 3, 4, 5, 6
Part C	1, 2, 3, 4, 5
Part D	7, 6, 5, 4, 3, 2, 1.

As in Example 4, patterns of pitch, and so on, could be superimposed. The same series could be used on different time-scales, as in Example 6, or the length of the patterns could be increased: 1, 1, 2, 1, 2, 3, 1, 2, 3, 4, 1, 2, 3, 4, 5, and so on.

Ex. 6

Example 7a uses a series of thirteen numbers drawn (approximately) on seven different time-scales, which are related by the geometrical progression 1, 2, 4, 8, 16,

32, 64. Example 7*b* shows a way of interpreting section 4 of Example 7*a*. The whole could be played under a conductor, but it is intended that players shall have their individual beat of approximately ♩ = 60, with no attempt at co-ordination in this respect.

Parts would be made up as follows. Each performer, with the aid of random numbers, or a pack of cards, decides (*a*) which patterns are to be played forward, and which are to be played backwards; and (*b*) the order of the patterns. Characteristics distinguishing the patterns are then noted (e.g. number 5, *staccato* and soft on one high note; number 4, continuous trills, etc.). Players may begin together, or in any order or interval of entry. Extra material may be added spontaneously as a reaction to other performers in this improvisation, which lasts about six minutes.

Ex. 7*a*

Ex. 7*b*

$\frac{4}{4}$ ♫ ♩ ♩ 𝄽 ♩ 𝄽 ♩ 𝄽 ♩ 𝄽 ♩ 𝄽 ♩ 𝄽 |etc.

([—2—] = 2 bars rest)

After working with this material it may be attempted again as a freer improvisation by a small group, with the idea only as a basis. One or more ostinato patterns, not necessarily related to the series, could be played by others.

Other number series may be exploited in similar ways. For example, the Fibonacci series: 1, 2, 3, 5, 8, 13, 21, etc., in which two adjacent terms add up to the following one. Much more interest may be obtained by permutating a series.

Bell patterns are a ready form of permutation:

Ex. 8

```
7 6 5 4 3 2 1
6 7 4 5 2 3 1
6 4 7 2 5 1 3
4 6 2 7 1 5 3
4 2 6 1 7 3 5
2 4 1 6 3 7 5
2 1 4 3 6 5 7  etc.
```

47

Ex. *8a*

Ex. *8b*

Ex. *8c*

Chime-bars could each be allotted a number (as in Example 8*a*) and the permutations played as a continuous chain (Example 8*b*). Alternatively, several permutations could be played together, with one pitch allotted to each, the numbers here indicating beats. Durations, volume, and so on, could be decided by individuals. Example 8*c* shows the bell-patterns in Example 8 used in this way.

Longer and shorter bell-patterns could be used in a similar manner, and a number could be employed simultaneously. Example 9 shows the outline of such a texture for thirty performers. The seven players of part 'd' play the material of Example 8*c* alternately forward (O) and retrograde (R), separating these with a silence equal to the length of the pattern. Parts 'a', 'b', 'c', and 'e' are for four, five, six, and eight performers respectively, and each is derived from a bell-pattern based on the number concerned. Parts 'a', 'b', 'c', 'd', and 'e' should be distinguished by tone-colour and/or position; some groups may use non-pitched instruments. There may be a conductor, but independent beats for the groups are feasible. Further details of performance might be left to the separate groups.

Ex. 9

Example 9 may be looked upon as a compound instance of Example 3, and further such instances may be related to Examples 5 and 6. The material employed need not necessarily be based on a number series or its permutations. Textures invented by the groups may be used.

Random numbers
These may be assigned as symbols to represent any elements of music. The music

resulting can only be analysed on a statistical basis. Two examples of their use are given: Ex. 10

A	2	3			I		I	3	I	2	2			3	I	I		I	2	I	4		I	2				2		2	I	2
B			I		I			I				I	I		I		2		I			I		2	I	I		I	I	
C								I																	I					
D																		I												
E																														
	01 02 03 04 05				09			13			17			21			25			29										

A	2	2		I		2	I	I	I	I	2			2	3		I		I	I	I	I	3	I	I
B	I	I		I	I	I		2	I		I	2		2	I		2		I		2
C	I		I		I	I			I		I				I
D					2						
E	I									
	33	37	41	45	49	53	57	61		

A	I	I	I	I	2		I	I		I	I		I	5		I		I	I	3	I	2	I	2	2	I	I	2
B	2			I			I	I	I	2	I		I	I	I	2	I
C	I		I		I	2		I		I	I
D		I		I		
E					
	65	69	73	77	81	85	89	93	97	00

1. THE POISSON DISTRIBUTION LAW

This describes 'the occurrence of isolated events in a continuum' (M. J. Moroney, *Facts from Figures*, Penguin, 1962). In Examples 10 and 11 the law is used to position events for five performers in a piece lasting 100 units of time (possibly seconds). This particular use of the law gives the number of events as:

PART A 100, PART B 50, PART C 17,

PART D 4 and PART E 1.

distributed as shown in the following table:

| PART A | TIME-UNITS | 37 | 18 | 6 | 1 | 1 | 37 |
| | EVENTS PER TIME-UNIT | 1 | 2 | 3 | 4 | 5 | 0 |

| PART B | TIME-UNITS | 30 | 10 | 60 |
| | EVENTS PER TIME–UNIT | 1 | 2 | 0 |

| PART C | TIME-UNITS | 15 | 1 | 84 |
| | EVENTS PER TIME-UNIT | 1 | 2 | 0 |

| PART D | TIME-UNITS | 4 | 96 |
| | EVENTS PER TIME-UNIT | 1 | 0 |

| PART E | TIME-UNITS | 1 | 99 |
| | EVENTS PER TIME-UNIT | 1 | 0 |

That is, in part A there will be one sound starting in each of 37 boxes of one time-unit each, two sounds in 18 boxes, and so on. Each box is given a two-figure number (01, 02, ... 98, 99, 00). A table of random numbers (readily available in books on statistics) is scanned in rows or columns, and the number '1' is inserted in the 37 boxes whose numbers first appear in the table, the number '2' in the 18 boxes whose numbers then appear, and so on. Example 10 shows one of many possible results. Each number indicates how many sounds start within a given time-unit. They may be converted into crotchets, quavers, etc., or the exact timing may be left to performers. Volume, pitch, instrumentation, etc., could be left free or defined. The position of some numbers could be given extra significance (for example, the sounds of part D could become the dividing points for a piece in five sections; Example 11a shows a possible harmonic structure for these, and Example 11b gives part of this harmonic structure in a piano layout of boxes 81–100 of Example 10, where random numbers have been used to assist the placing of pitches).

Ex. 11a

Ex. 11b

51

Example 12 is part of a piece derived by a student from a similar layout to Example 10. In parts A, B, and D each event is one sound. But in part C each event is three sounds, and part E is represented by a broken trill starting at the time indicated by the positioning of the one event and continuing to the end of the piece.

Ex. 12

Longer pieces could be made by using the layout, or parts of it, several times in succession and/or combination; variety being obtained by interchanging the parts, altering the time-scale, using several versions together of part B only, varying the instrumentation, and so on.

2. AN APPLICATION OF RANDOM NUMBERS TO THE CONSTRUCTION OF A SHORT SECTIONAL PIECE

Use is made of the Fibonacci sequence 1, 2, 3, 5, 8, etc.

(i) Preliminary decisions
   (*a*) There are to be eight performers — glockenspiel, xylophone, two chime-bar players, melodica, drums, cymbals, wood-blocks.
   (*b*) The piece is to have five sections.
   (*c*) The durations of the sections are to be — 10, 20, 30, 50, and 80 seconds. (For practical purposes the piece is divided into 'bars' of four seconds' duration.)
   (*d*) The number of performers in a section is to be 1, 2, 3, 5 or 8.
(ii) The following decisions are made with the aid of a table of random numbers:
   (*e*) The lengths of the sections in order.
   (*f*) The number of performers per section in order.

(g) Description of the performers for successive sections.
(h) The average number of sounds per second for each section.
(i) The relative density of attacks for each performer.
The results of this working are given in the table below:

Number of section (b)		1	2	3	4	5
Duration in seconds (c)		20	10	30	80	50
Duration in bars (c)		5	2½	4½	20	12½
Number of players (d), (f)		1	2	5	8	3
Glockenspiel		—	—	$^3/_{10}$	$^1/_8$	—
Xylophone		—	—	$^2/_{10}$	$^1/_8$	$^3/_6$
Chime-bars A		$^1/_1$	—	—	$^1/_8$	—
Chime-bars B	(g)	—	—	$^1/_{10}$	$^1/_8$	$^2/_6$
Melodica		—	—	—	$^1/_8$	—
Drums		—	$^2/_3$	$^3/_{10}$	$^1/_8$	—
Cymbals		—	—	$^1/_{10}$	$^1/_8$	$^1/_6$
Wood-blocks		—	$^1/_3$	—	$^1/_8$	—
Average density (h)		1½	½	4	1	2½
Theoretical number of attacks (i)		30	5	120	80	125

Chime-bars A and B refer to the pitches used, and both performers are involved in each case. At each stage in which random numbers are used the concept of the piece in detail is altered. Sometimes chance leads to a situation which cannot be conceived in practice, in which case it should be rejected. But more frequently one is stimulated by the possibility of an unusual situation.

(iii) *Time-intervals between attacks*
It was decided to have the following:

20 time intervals of ¼ time-unit
24   ”   ”   ½   ”
19   ”   ”   1   ”
12   ”   ”   2   ”
5   ”   ”   4   ”

By means of random numbers these are arranged in a fixed succession as shown below:

¼ 2 ½ 1 ½ ¼ ¼ ½ ¼ 1 1 ¼ ½ 1 1 ¼ 1 ¼ ½ ¼

1 2 ½ ¼ 2 ¼ 2 2 ½ 1 2 1 1 ¼ 2 ½ 2 4 ¼ 1

¼ ½ ¼ 1 2 ¼ ½ ¼ ½ 1 2 2 1 ¼ 2 1 ¼ 2 ½ 2

4 ½ ¼ 1 1 1 1 ½ 1 2 ¼ ½ 1 ½ ¼ ¼ ½ ½ ¼ 1

The scale on which these numbers are used depends on the density required for a given section. The beginning of the table is laid out below, firstly with the time-unit equal to one second, and then as actually used for a density of 1½ sounds per second in section one of the piece.

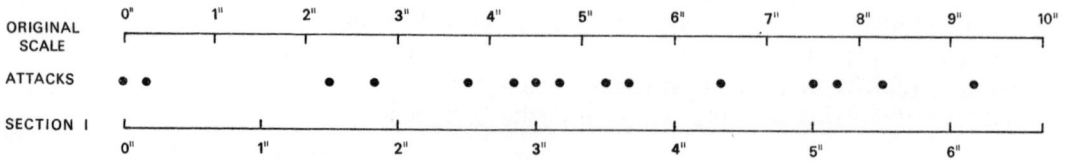

The random-number table is used to determine which attacks are allotted to which instruments, according to the proportions required. The actual number of attacks is close to but not identical with the theoretical number because of the employment of random numbers.

Ex. 13a

Ex. 13b

(iv) Pitch

A sequence of pitches derived from a Fibonacci sequence, together with its inversion (Example 13a) is the origin of the pitches actually used (Example 13b). Within these limits pitch is decided by the use of random numbers to maintain an approximately equal distribution of each pitch throughout a section. But among a number of exceptions to this were:

Section 1. The entry of D sharp and A flat were delayed and deliberately introduced in diads (two-note chords).

Section 3. It is mostly arranged that a pitch occurs three times before more random entries (a similar principle is applied to drums and cymbals).

Section 4. The diads are arranged in palindrome-like series of intervals. For example, the glockenspiel: minor third, major third, minor second, diminished fifth, minor second, major third and minor third. The lengths of tremolos and the melodica sounds are mostly decided on by the occurrence of a certain number of attacks after their starts.

Section 5. There is a deliberate reduction in the number of pitches until only one is left for each instrument. This was planned to echo the diminished fifth which had arrived randomly at the beginning. Repetition of notes in the xylophone part was avoided until all pitches were eliminated but the A flat.

In the completed piece given in Example 14 the type of attack used in the various instruments is partly to accentuate the differences in the five sections.

This detailed working-out gives the composer a great deal of satisfaction, and the performers a task demanding concentrated practice and development of skill.

Ex. 14

Ex. 14 (cont.)

Glockenspiel
Xylophone
Chime-Bars
Alto Melodica
Drums
Cymbals
Wood-Blocks
p cresc.
p cresc.
p cresc.
p cresc.
IV
Hard sticks
f vibrato where possible
Brush
Brush
V
Soft sticks
pp vibrato
Felt sticks
Metal stick

Ex. 14 (cont.)

The following are four successive simplifications of the piece. The original demands no creative ability on the part of the performers, and much labour on the part of the composer. The successive simplifications demand less detail from the composer and increased creativity from performers.

1

	0″	20″	30″	60″	140″	190″
GL			1:1 ●	1:8 ～～		
XY			1:1 ●	1:8 ～～	1+:1 ●	
CH (X2)	1:1 ～～		1:5	1:8 ～～	1−:1 ～～	
MEL				1:8 ●		
DR		2:10 ●	1+:1 ●	1:8 ～～ | ●		
CY			1+:3 ●	1:8 ～～ | ●	1:2½	
WB		1:10 ●		1:8 ～～ | ●		

(ratios example 1:5 = approx. one sound in 5 secs. average).

2.

	1	2	3	4	5
GL			1	2,3	
XY			1	2,3	1
CH (X2)	1		2	3,4	1
MEL				1	
DR		1	1	1,2	
CY			1	1,2	1,3
WB		1		1,2	

57

(section lengths not defined. Numbers to be interpreted as types of attack chosen individually by the players. Change of section indicated by a conductor or by arrangement among the players.)

3.

```
A          pause    x      y,z    pause
B          pause    x      y,z    x
C and D    w      pause    x  y,z     w
E          pause      x         pause
F          pause  x    x      x,y      pause
G          pause    x         x,y      x,z
H          pause    x   pause   x,y    pause
```

(Performers select their own sound-sources. No sectional co-ordination is indicated. Duration free.)

4. *'Five to ten performers play for one or two periods of time during a given three minutes. Each performer may make from none to three changes of attack.'*

The examples given indicate some of the possible links of music with mathematics. Beginning with the use of Cuisenaire rods in the infant school, there are many mathematical topics which make an excellent starting point for musical creation. As examples, take the following headings from the first three books of the School Mathematics Project (Cambridge University Press, 1965):

Book 1	Ch. 2	Sets
	Ch. 6	Number Patterns
	Ch. 7	Sequences and Relations
	Ch. 13	Symmetry
Book 2	Ch. 3	Similarity and Enlargement
	Ch. 5	Reflection and Rotation
	Ch. 6	Number Patterns
	Ch. 7	Translations and Vectors
Book 3	Ch. 1	Probabilities
	Ch. 2	Isometrics
	Ch. 3	Matrices
	Ch. 6	Networks
	Ch. 11	Identity and Inverse

FURTHER READING

Formalized Music: Thought and Mathematics in Composition by Iannis Xenakis (Indiana University Press, 1972)

The Mathematical Basis of the Arts by Joseph Schillinger (Johnson Reprint Corporation, USA, 1966)

7. Group work and the music of some twentieth-century composers

It is essential that some time is set apart for listening to music. The shortcomings of traditional 'musical appreciation' approaches are now widely acknowledged, and, in any case, the idea of quoting subjects, themes, developments, and so on, is often irrelevant to modern works, where individual pieces tend to have their own form and one that is frequently derived from the actual musical content. Generally speaking, group performances of twentieth-century music will be limited to educational works that demand limited technical resources, and some other works where instructions are verbal or graphic. The fact that the mainstream of modern music is technically beyond the reach of many people in terms of performance does not mean, however, that listening cannot be vastly enriched by creating situations that demand involvement in depth. This section is devoted to ways of encouraging such involvement.

Piece derived from Bartók

Ex. 1

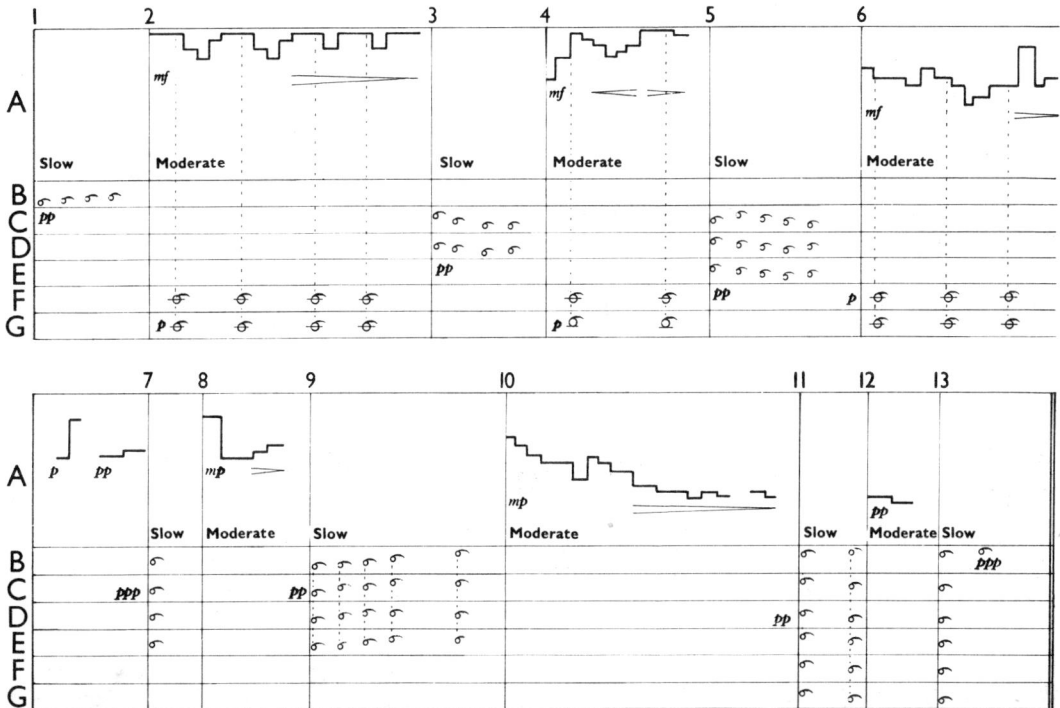

Example 1 is distributed for performance by a group Part A is presented graphically, with pitch (vertical) and time (horizontal) drawn to scale. If more than one player (or singer) is to be employed, the phrases would be allocated as solos.

Parts B, C, D and E. One or more players to each part (if only two players are available, each player may perform two parts). The shapes of melodic movement are indicated. Possibly glockenspiels may be used.

Parts F and G: lower in pitch than parts B–E. One note for each performer in Part F, and two notes for each performer in part G.

The performance could be held together by signals given by the conductor at the given numbers, or without any conductor, after suitable rehearsal. In either case, two 'lead' players would have to be appointed, one for group B–E and the other for group F–G. The lead player of the group F–G would observe carefully the progress of Part A as it follows roughly the time and pitch indicated by the graph.

Ex. 2   BÉLA BARTÓK   *Ten Easy Pieces: Dedication*

When a reasonable version has been performed, everyone listens to Example 2, from which Example 1 was derived. Discuss the group version and Bartók's original, together with the form and the way the chord sections develop. Perform from the graph again and invite ideas for improvisation that are based on some aspect of the piece – a solo with a group or groups, two or more groups without a solo, one group expanding in volume or in number of performers, or changing its position in space (expanding or moving as a compact whole), with another group improvising freely and a third group contracting in time, in space, in pitch, and so on.

By these means the members of the group will have attained an insight into the composing process by repetition, adaptation (skill will be required of the teacher in deciding how much to influence the diagram interpretation), and by musical invention. They will also have become better listeners and, one hopes, will listen more and need guidance less.

Piece derived from Webern

Ex. 3

In Example 3, the whole of part A may be allocated to one player (or singer), or the phrases may be divided between several performers. Parts B, C, D and E could be performed by chime-bars, glockenspiels, guitars, piano (on the keys and/or plucking the strings), or other instruments. The teacher may ask for high, repeated notes, or this may be left to be discovered later by the pupils. There could be more than one performer per part. Similarly, two or more players could be employed on any of the unpitched parts, which should be delicately played, involving the use of wire brushes or fingers rather than beaters. The conductor would divide the beats.

Ex. 4   ANTON WEBERN   *Five Pieces for Orchestra, Op. 10*

III

Sehr langsam und äußerst ruhig ($\quad$ = ca 40)

Kl. in B

Hr. in F
m. Dpf.

espress.
pp

Pos.
m. Dpf.

Harmon.

Mand.
ppp   *dim.*   *verklingend*

Git.
ppp   *dim.*   *verklingend*

Cel.
ppp   *dim.*   *verklingend*

Hrf.
ppp   *dim.*   *verklingend*

gr. Tr.
tr
kaum hörbar

kl. Tr.

Glocken
einige tiefe
kaum hörbar   *verklingend*

Herden-
glocken
continuierlich mit vielen Glocken
kaum hörbar   *verklingend*

Sehr langsam und äußerst ruhig ($\quad$ = ca 40)

Solo - Gg.
o. Dpf.
G-Saite
dolce
pp   *pp*

Solo - Br.
m. Dpf.

Solo - Vlc.
m. Dpf.

U. E. 5967 / U. E. 12416

zögernd
drängend - - zögernd molto rit. - - - tempo
5 molto espr.
Kl. in B
Hr. in F m. Dpf.
Pos. m. Dpf.
Harmon.
Mand.
Git.
Cel.
Hrf.
gr. Tr.
kl. Tr.
Glocken
kaum hörbar
äußerst leise
Herden-glocken
kaum hörbar
zögernd
drängend - - zögernd molto rit. - - - tempo
Solo - Gg. o. Dpf.
dolcissimo
Solo - Br. m. Dpf.
pizz. (vibrato)
arco
Solo - Vlc. m. Dpf.

Ex. 4 (cont.)

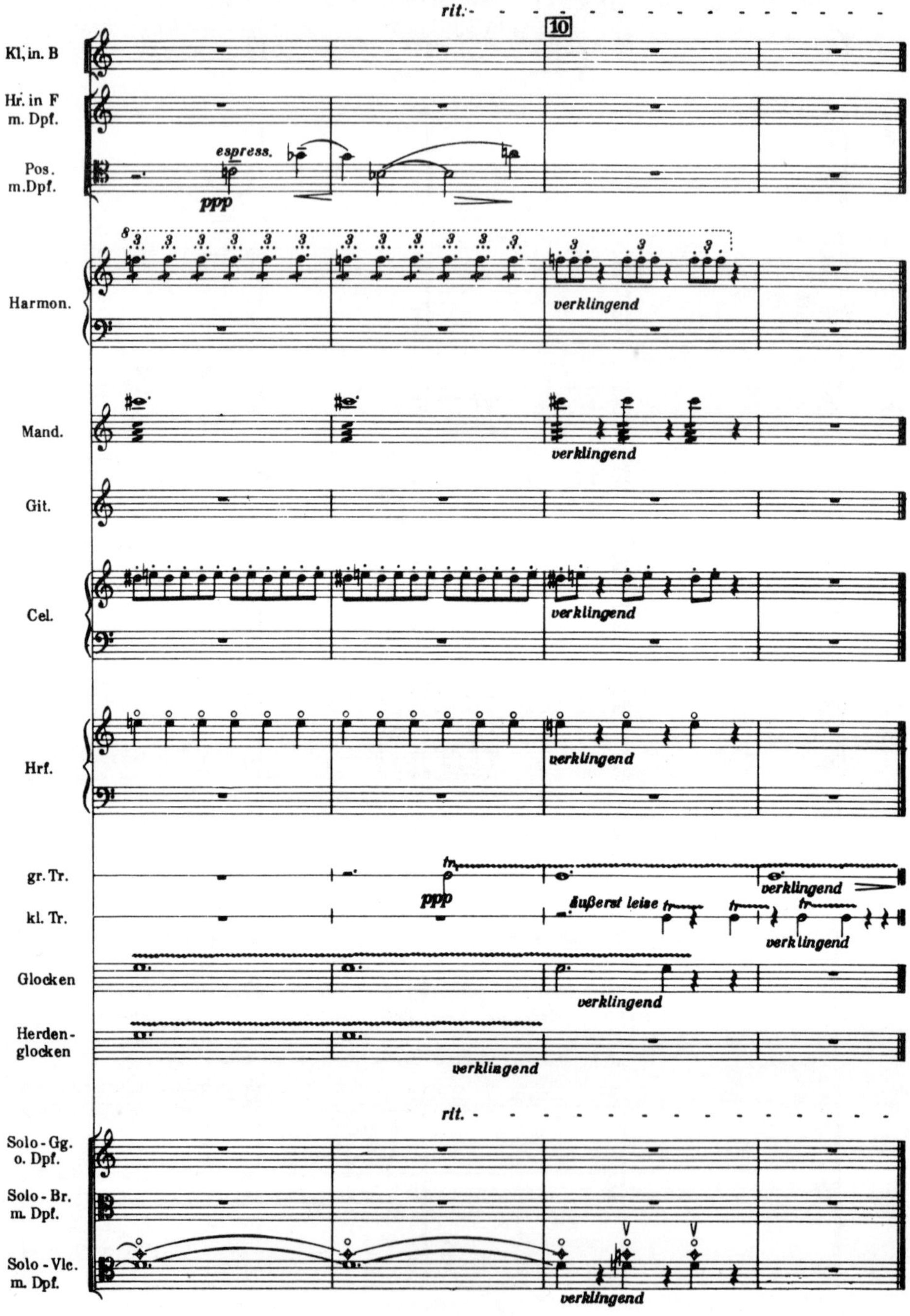

U.E. 5967 / U.E. 12416

After a number of rehearsals, listen to Webern's original (Example 4) while following the diagram. In the ensuing discussion, it is likely to be revealed that someone has noticed the missing melodic shapes in bars 8 and 9. Perform the piece again, trying to complete the parts.

The barring of Example 3 does not conform with that of Example 4, as the former was designed primarily for those who lack skill in reading, and simplicity was therefore essential.

Accents at the beginning of bars should of course be avoided unless indicated.

Further work with Webern

Much of Webern's later work consists of interlocking fragments. Some practical involvement for the prospective listener is particularly useful here, as children in particular are familiar with song and its long, flowing lines. Example 5 shows the opening of the String Quartet, Op. 28 (Universal Edition Ph.390), arranged for five chime-bar players. The register of some of the notes has been changed, but the pitch, shape and rhythm have been retained.

Part A — 2 notes = violin 1.
Part B — 3 notes = violin 2.
Parts C and D — 2 notes each = viola.
Part E — 3 notes = 'cello.

Ex. 5

Staccato sounds should be dampened immediately (*pizz.*) and other sounds dampened at least at the end of a group. A visual impression of the twelve-note row

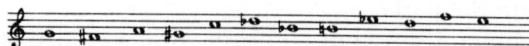

may be given by seating the players in the order C A B E D. This visual impression is destroyed with the inversion of the row beginning in bar 7, but the original row occurs again, beginning with player C in bar 10. The last two notes of this version (Player D, bar 11) become the first two notes of the original row transposed down a tone, at the conclusion of which the extract ends.

A performance such as this is useful in showing the structure of the music, but it should be made clear to the group that the parts are not restricted to these notes later in the quartet, although the ordering of the notes is always related to the original row.

As an additional basis for work with note-rows the rearrangement of the bars of melodic percussion instruments that permit this may be considered. The original row of Webern's Op. 28 might be arranged thus on a 20-note instrument, retaining a 'keyboard' shape:

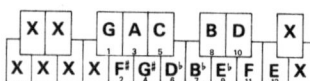

Alternatively, the positions of the 'white' notes only could be used. A transposition of the row would appear thus:

In either case, players could produce retrograde forms simply by playing from right to left. Other players could set up inversions of the row in a similar fashion and provide retrograde inversions also. With variation in duration and volume, the positioning of pauses, single sounds, repeated sounds, tremolos, chords on adjacent notes, and with the adoption of the second layout above, *glissandi*, there is much scope for improvisation. Groups of three notes only could be abandoned and other ideas, not normally a part of twelve-note technique, are likely to be forthcoming. Pupils can invent their own rows, and the redistribution and use of all twenty notes on these instruments appears as a logical development.

Webern's Concerto, Op. 24

The beginning of the *Concerto*, Op. 24, by Webern (Example 6) shows the exposition of its row in groups of three overlapping sounds by wind instruments, each group played at a different speed. The piano answers with the groups, speeds and phrasing in reverse order.

Ex. 6 ANTON WEBERN *Concerto, Op. 24*

I

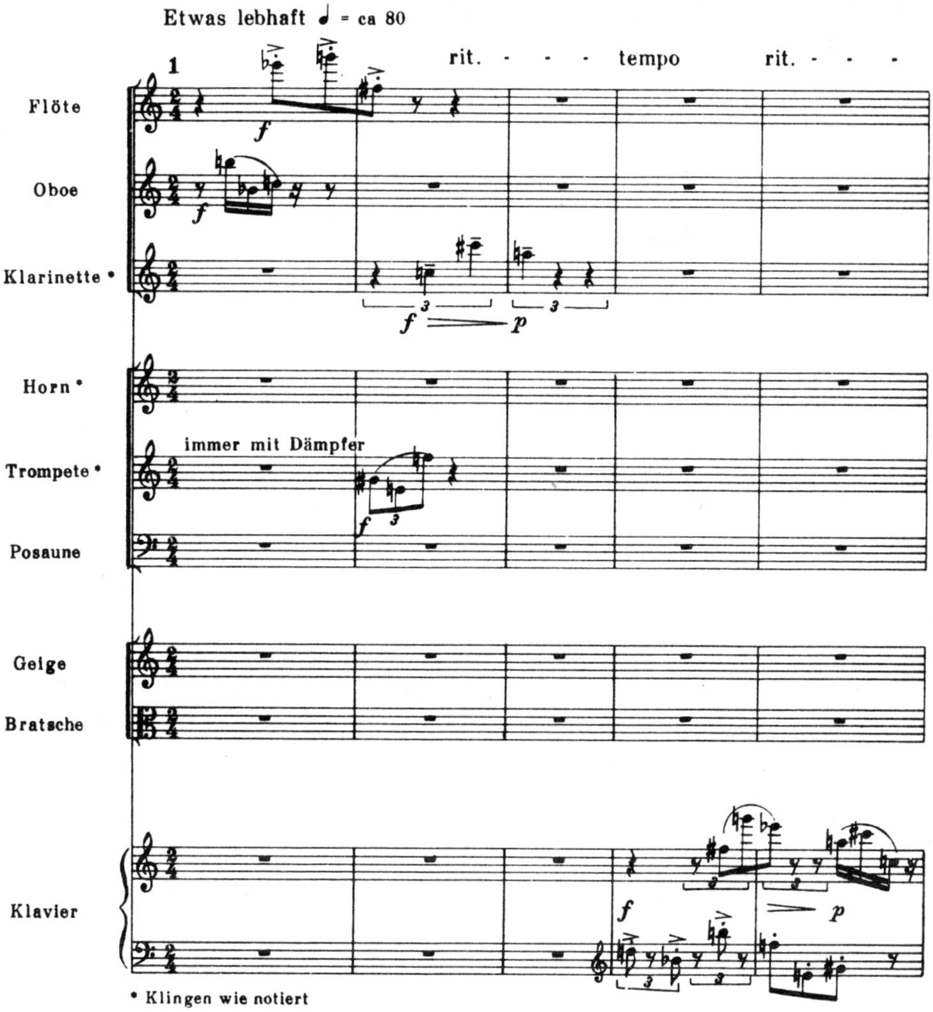

This could be performed, with approximate rhythm, by four players with three chime-bars each — staff notation could be used, or the terms 'high', 'middle' and 'low'. A common notation for each may however simplify matters, using L = left, C = centre and R = right, according to the position of the bars laid out in the order of the row (see Example 7a). Thus the 'wind instrument' part:

Player 1	L C R
Player 2	L C R
Player 3	L C R
Player 4	L C R

is answered by the 'piano' part:

Player 1	R C L
Player 2	R C L
Player 3	R C L
Player 4	R C L

Ex. 7

Original→   ←Retrograde

(a)

L   C   R   L   C   R   L   C   R   L   C   R

Retrogade inversion→   ←Inversion

R   C   L   R   C   L   R   C   L   R   C   L
player ①   player ②   player ③   player ④

(b)

O   RI   R   RI

(c)

L C R │ R C L │ RC L │ R CL │ L CR │ LC   R   │
   f   p   f   p   p   f   f   p

(d)

Example *7a* shows the retrograde and inversion forms easily available to the same players. By adding the use of alternate double and single notes (LC R, L CR, R CL and RC L), further changes in rhythm, volume and *staccato*, the use of two rows of different transposition simultaneously, and so on, it is possible to simulate the chief devices of the piece. Furthermore, if xylophone bars can be lined up with the chime-bars, tone-colour contrasts also become available. Improvisation with all of these devices will serve as excellent preparation for listening to the concerto.

Allowing for transposition, this particular row may be considered as a row of only three notes, in four different forms (Example *7b*). If, then, we acknowledge each player as possessing a full row, the four players may function independently during a group improvisation. A scheme such as that in Example *7c* may be used as a start. Each player would begin when he desires, judging the length of the pauses according to the activity of the other performers (for example, an attempt would be made to delay the entry of soft sounds until it could be reasonably anticipated that they would be heard). Another version could allow the players to perform the events in any order, and this leads to permutation of the note-order within an event – LCR LRC RCL RLC CRL CLR (here we are moving away from Webern).

With a twenty-note range of chime-bars six players could next be accommodated using the same intervals (Example *7d*). Further work could consist of using other twelve-note rows, the notes being selected by the players themselves, abandoning the twelve-note row and allowing duplication of notes, increasing the number of notes per player (omitting some in the course of the improvisations), and introducing unpitched instruments (for example, wood-blocks in the order middle, high, low, instead of B B♭ D, in Example *7b*). There are limitless ways in which written compositions (in musical notation, graph notation, diagrams, words, etc.) and improvisations could develop from this work.

Work with Penderecki

Ex. *8a*

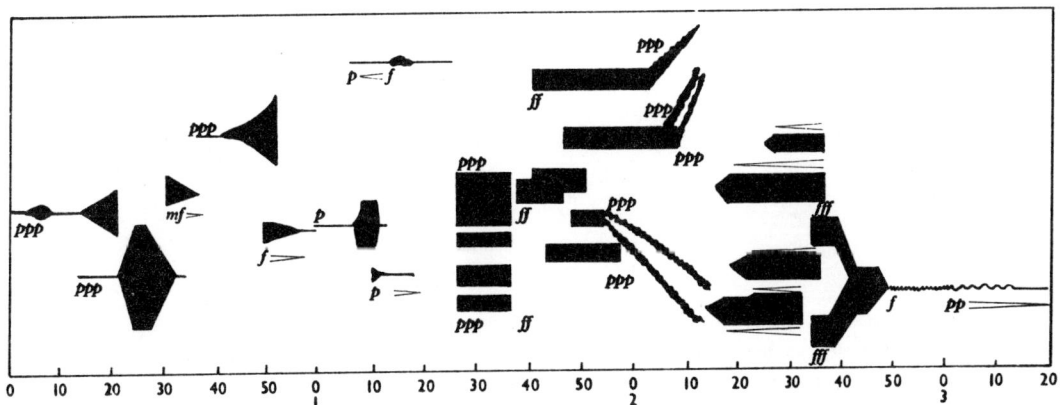

Ex. 8b

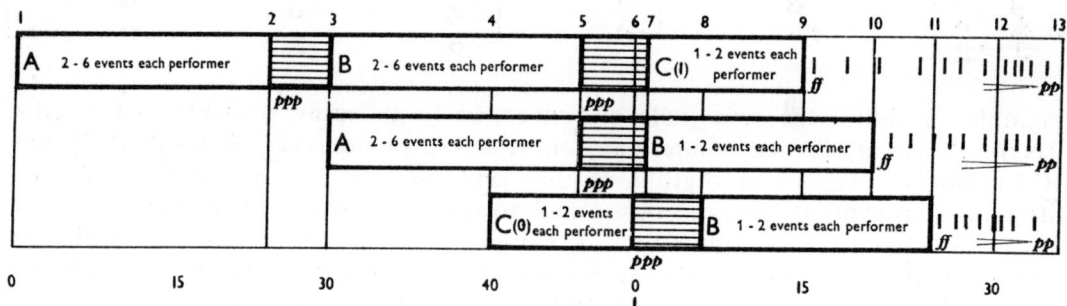

Penderecki's *Threnody: To the Victims of Hiroshima,* for fifty-two stringed instruments, begins with very high-pitched long sounds with varying vibrato, leading to one minute of rapid, freely timed, indeterminate sounds — tapping the sounding board, playing between the bridge and tailpiece, and so on. The third section, which overlaps by about five seconds with the previous one, consists of clusters of sound of various sizes, adjacent instruments in the clusters being one quarter-tone apart. This section is drawn to scale as to pitch and time in Example 8a. The quality of tone of the blocks of sound differs with the instruments employed and with the attack used — with or without mutes, *sul ponticello,* tremolo harmonics *glissando* (at '2 minutes' in the diagram), and with vibrato (at 2′45″ a unison sound with fast vibrato, then slow vibrato, and finally non-vibrato). The blocks at 2′10″ begin with accented attacks. For a listener, the diagram shows the intentions of the composer better than the score. Such diagrams are invaluable for claiming the attention of even the most unmusical to a recording of a work such as this. Concentration may be further increased by stopping the tape and asking for the position in time on the graph or by asking for a show of hands at various events.

Drawn on a larger scale in both dimensions, this diagram could easily be adapted for class performance. For a class of thirty, divide the diagram horizontally into thirty parts. With one pitch for each player. Notes could be allocated chromatically:

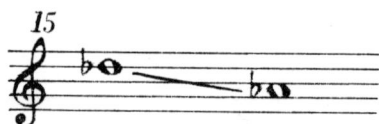

Players 1 – 6 glockenspiels

Players 7 – 30 chime-bars

Volume would be very important, and attack could consist of fast, repeated sounds (with rubber and wood beaters for the chime-bar players), and rubbing the bars with a beater. At 2′45″ a vibro-card (see *New Sounds in Class*) could be used on the chime-bars.

70

With the players arranged in a semi-circle, one or more conductors could improvise a piece on the same lines. Such an experiment could begin with a conductor pointing to one player to start, moving his right arm clockwise while keeping the left stationary, and following this with a movement of the left arm to meet the right. Assuming the player of the highest pitched sound to be on the conductor's left, the following pattern would emerge:

Overlapping with this may be another pattern formed by another conductor. Graphs could also be drawn by pupils, the best of these being selected for performance, or lettering stencils could possibly be used, and also those employed for drawing chemical and electronic apparatus.

The fourth section of *Threnody* is a canon for three orchestras of twelve players each. This is represented schematically in Example 8*b*. Each sub-section is separated by a *pianissimo* chord (played tremolo, *sul ponticello* and *col legno*). It would seem that the invention of a canon is only one of a number of suitable means for obtaining the required texture, which consists of *staccato* sounds with a variety of attack, together with longer sounds of up to three seconds' duration (tremolo, harmonics, etc.). Thus, at signal 4 in Example 8*b* thirty-six parts, independent in pitch, attack and rhythm, are in progress. (It should be stated that Penderecki's music is here written in 2/4, but this is too complicated to reproduce for educational purposes.) The ending of the section consists of varied, short attacks with independent rhythms in the three orchestras but unison attack within each orchestra. This section overlaps here with the fifth and last section, consisting of further cluster chords, initially accompanied by arhythmic effects in the bass instruments.

Example 8*b* could be used with a large class divided into three equal groups, but the canon would be ignored. Pitched and non-pitched instruments and voices could be employed. The events, in number as suggested in the example, should be freely timed and well contrasted, each consisting of one sound, and occasionally two. Most events will be *staccato*, but longer sounds of up to three seconds are also needed, with a larger proportion of these in A than in B or C. The concerted attacks at the end would be timed by the three group-leaders, and the effects occurring simultaneously in any one group should be the same.

Possibly canons could next be devised that consist of strongly contrasted events within the capability of the voices and instruments available. As an example, take the following, which is suitable for melodic percussion and piano:

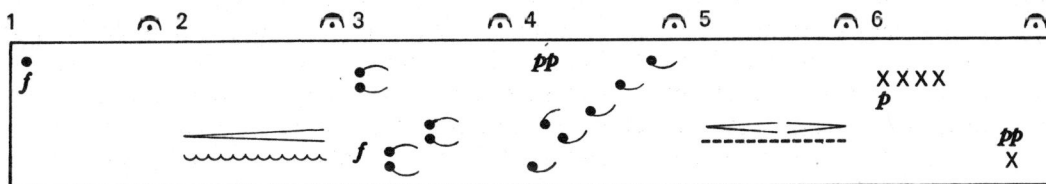

Pitch shape is indicated and unpitched sounds are denoted by crosses. Each performer could realize this in a number of ways, including:

(*a*) All entries indicated by a conductor.

(*b*) Entries of performers in a fixed order without a conductor, each entry timed with a certain event reached by the preceding performer (for example, each entry could be timed to coincide with a different entry of the preceding performer).

(*c*) Free entries, with speeds, pauses between repetitions and pauses within the events, decided by individual players.

(*d*) Variations — retrograde, inversion, retrograde, inversion, permutation, repetition of events, addition to and subtraction from events, omission of events, addition of other events, change of dynamics and speed (*ppp.* to *fff.*, *accel.* to *rit.*) and so on.

Small groups could invent their own canons and all groups could then play their canons together, with some suitable direction from the tutor.

Work with Lutoslawski

Ex. 9

	1	2	3	4
Woodwind				
Brass				
Percussion				
Timpani				
Piano				
Strings	12"	27"	18"	21"

	5 6 7	8	9 10 11 12
Woodwind			
Brass			
Percussion			
Timpani			
Piano			
Strings	6" 2" 24"	39"	

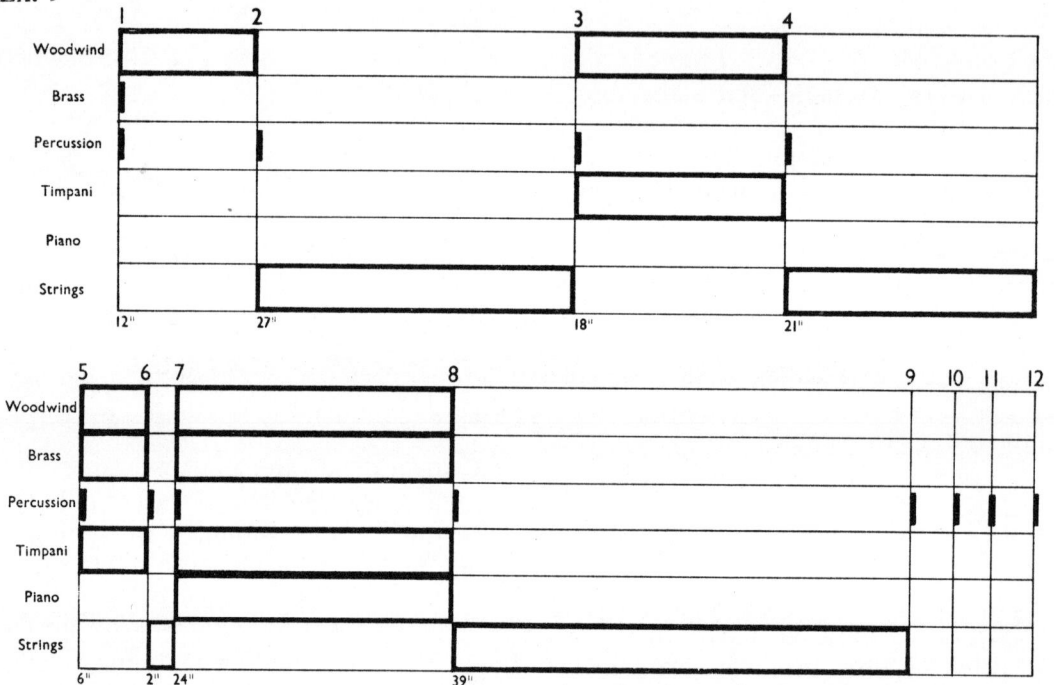

Jeux Vénitiens by Lutoslawski (Moeck), for large orchestra, is in four movements. The first has characteristics of figuration and regular growth which occur in all the movements. It is shown schematically in Example 9, where the alternation of strings with woodwind plus a growing succession of other groups can be seen. The material for each performer is exactly written as separate parts, but no detailed time-relationship between one part and another is laid down. The conductor signals the beginning and end of each section and players repeat material as necessary between these signals. Regular growth is shown in the details of the parts; piano part 1 has chords separated by silences of increasing length, piano part 2 has chords separated by silences of decreasing length. Repeated notes, played *accelerando*, are accompanied mostly by

72

static chords, and the florid woodwind parts, besides showing such speed changes in a freer way, anticipate the style of the flute solo of the third movement. The short, trill-like groups of the brass are used again in movements 2 and 4. Pupils should perform from the diagram, with available instrumentation, before and after listening to the recording.

Ex. 10

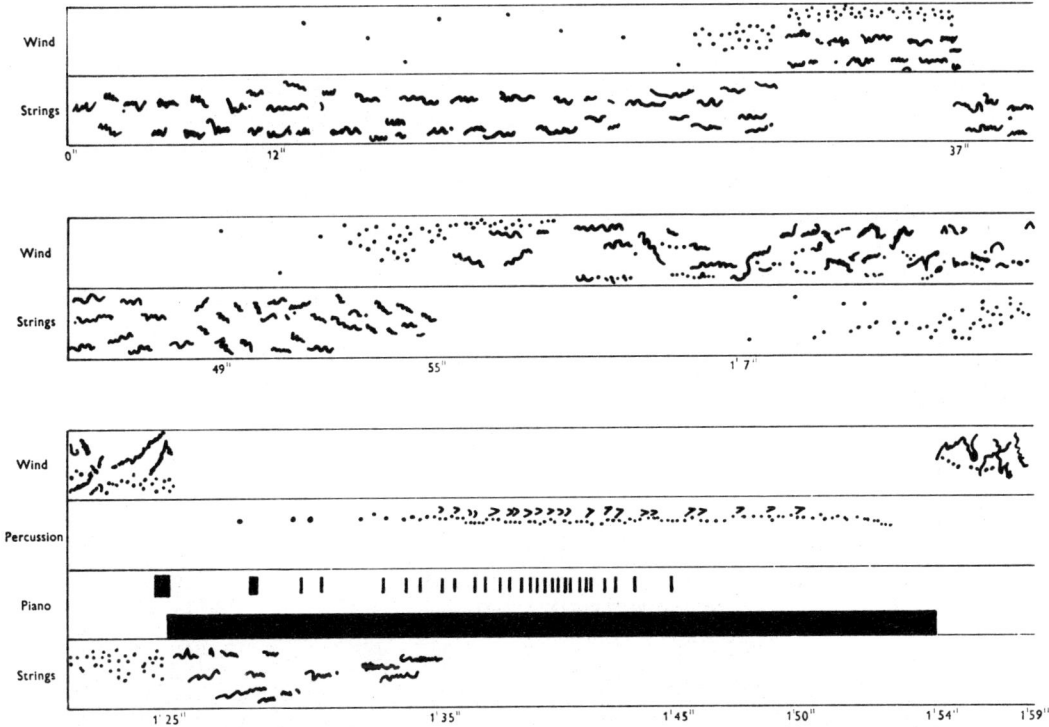

The second movement is shown schematically in Example 10. It is quiet throughout and the 'squiggles' represent fast groups of notes of varying length. Increases of speed in the wind and string parts, the increase and decrease of speed in the clusters of piano part No. 1, and the regular increase of speed and reduction of accentuation in the percussion parts are clearly shown. This movement again may be simulated by the pupils before and after listening.

Movement 3 is a flute solo of an improvisatory character with soft, resonant, decorated 'backing'. Apart from the string parts, which play *staccato* chords, first *accelerando* and then *ritardando*, the movement does not lend itself to a diagram layout. Movement 4 could well be represented by a diagram, and the idea of growth is so prominent here that pupils might themselves attempt a diagram of the whole or part of the movement.

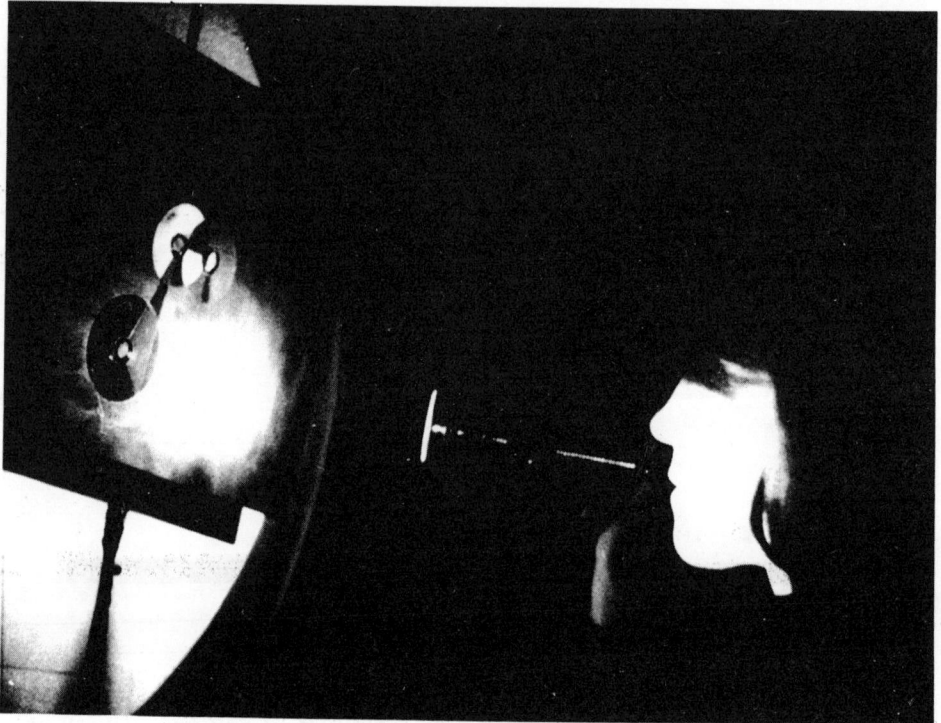

Torch shining on photoresistor cells. See *Making Simple Equipment* p. 75

8. Electronic equipment

The following notes may provide a useful starting point for musicians who possess no technical knowledge and for whom a much-needed book on the subject has yet to be published. Emphasis is placed more on the making and connecting of equipment than on its manipulation, which will vary according to the inclinations, understanding and experience of the individual.

MAKING SIMPLE EQUIPMENT

A great deal of pleasure is to be derived from making simple equipment and finding special uses for it. Most of the circuits discussed in this section resulted from a fascination with the idea of audience-participation in a hall where sounds were controlled, to various extents, by the shining of torches on photoresistor cells. No doubt more efficient instruments could have been designed by electronics experts, but rather crude sound was preferred, in this instance, to the more polished variety obtainable from sophisticated equipment. Furthermore, some satisfaction was derived from such positive application of one's technical limitations.

(a) Some sources of information

CATALOGUES

The best of these are a mine of information and a charge is made for them. Two suggestions are those of Henry's Radio Ltd, 303 Edgware Road, London W2 1BN (as well as listing a wide range of components and equipment the catalogue gives some circuits and the connection configurations of various transistors); and R.S. Components Ltd, 13–17 Epworth Street, London EC2P 2HA (supplies the trade and educational establishments but not individuals – very quick delivery service).

MAGAZINES

Subscription to a few magazines is invaluable, not only for the articles but also for the advertisements, where it will be seen that although prices of individual items may vary considerably from one dealer to another, considerable reductions may sometimes be obtained by buying in bulk. It is unfortunate that the only magazine to deal more or less exclusively with audio equipment (*Studio Sound*) considers mostly very large and expensive equipment beyond the normal purchasing power of schools and colleges. *Everyday Electronics* and *Practical Electronics* give useful circuits with full details of construction. *Wireless World* is more sophisticated. Occasional items of interest to the musician will be found in *Electronics Today, Practical Wireless*, and *The Home Constructor.*

All these magazines are issued monthly, and it seems to be quite common for errors in circuits to be corrected one or more issues later. Interesting modifications may be suggested even six months or a year later in correspondence columns.

BOOKS

Questions and Answers on Electronics by Clement Brown (George Newnes, 1967). A
   useful general background book.

Using Semiconductors by John Hughes and Thomas M. Johnston (Heinemann Educational Books, 1970): electronics to 'O' Level standard.

The following may be very useful despite their high degree of technicality:

Basic Electronics for Scientists by J. P. Brophy (McGraw Hill, 1966)

Pulse Digital and Switching Waveforms by J. Millman and H. Taub (McGraw Hill, 1965)

Elektronische Musik in der Schule by Rudolf E. Hagen (Universal Edition, 1972).

MULLARD EDUCATIONAL SERVICE PUBLICATIONS
(Mullard House, Torrington Place, London WC1E 7HD)

Simple Transistor Measurements

Educational Electronic Experiments (includes amplifier/oscillator, low-voltage D.C. supply, and a very simple electronic organ).

Useful Ideas (includes a multivibrator, a square-wave convertor, an electronic metronome and a sine-wave generator).

Circards (Wireless World), especially:

Series 1: *Basic Active Filters*

Series 3: *Waveform Generators*

Series 5: *Audio Circuits.*

(b) Equipment

Multicore solder and a soldering iron with a 5/32" bit

'Tin' the iron before use by rubbing solder on the end of the bit as the iron warms. Apply the soldering iron and the solder to the joint at the same time, carefully but not too slowly. Rub the bit on a cloth after each joint is made.

Long-nosed pliers, small edge-cutters, wire-strippers, a small vice, and *a small screwdriver.*

Aluminium clips, for attachment to the transistor leads as protection while soldering.

For making holes in small aluminium boxes: *a small punch, hammer, rat-tail file, small flat file,* and a *hand drill.* A number of Q-Max punches would be a worthwhile investment for making holes neatly and quickly for various sockets and controls.

A *small multimeter* for making simple measurements and for testing continuity.

A resistance substitution box

Decs

Much time and labour may be saved by setting up and testing a circuit with solderless connections before the final assembly is attempted. The easiest boards for this purpose are S-Decs (all Decs obtainable from Morris Laboratory Instruments, 96–98 High Street, London SW15 1RD). These are plastic boxes the tops of which are pierced with lines of holes connected below by metal strips. Component leads may easily be inserted in these, and the box and components used again and again. Holders will have to be adapted, however, to accommodate transistors which have short leads. These holders would be unnecessary if T-Decs or U-Decs were used, for the holes in these are much closer together. These boards are most useful for integrated circuits, but small adapters will be required to link the integrated circuit holders to the board. It is useful to have one or two Decs glued to a wooden platform, and via a block of polythene terminals to make connections to an input socket and an output plug as well as battery connections. Two 4.5 batteries connected in series make it possible to have earth connection and a plus or minus 9 volts arrangement, or a centre earth connection with both plus and minus 4.5 volts (see Diagram 1).

Diagram 1

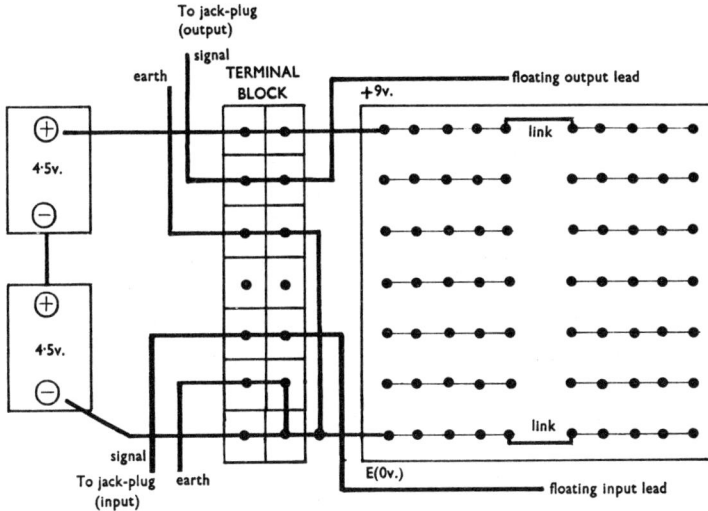

(c) Components
Initial expenditure on a reasonable collection of components will save numerous frustrating journeys to the local shop as it will frequently be found that the one resistor or capacitor required is not in stock at the time it is needed.

Capacitors: 0.01 microfarad, 0.1 microfarad. In a circuit these may be connected either way round (symbol ⊣⊢). For 1.0, 4.7, 10, 25, 47 and 100 microfarad electrolytic capacitors, low-voltage rating is again normally satisfactory. The positive end is indicated by a + sign, by a black or red mark, or by a ridge on the container (⊣▮⊢).

Resistors: Purchase a few of, say, six values in each decade from 10 ohms to 5.6 megohms (symbol —⋀⋀⋀—). Five per cent accuracy rated at ½ or ¼ watt are generally useful. Variable resistors — 5 kohm, 100 kohm, 500 kohm and 1 megohm (symbol ⋀⋀⋀⋀). In many cases only the centre contact and one other need be used. Log. and Lin. types are best suited to different places, but either may be used. It may be advisable to obtain Log. ones first.

Transistors: BC 107 and BC 109 serve many purposes. They are quite cheap when purchased twenty-five or more at a time. These are npn-transistors. Check with a catalogue for pin configuration and near equivalents (symbol   ); pnp transistors are less necessary initially (symbol   ). If you decide to experiment with the opposite type in a circuit, reverse the battery polarity. It is remarkable how many circuits use transistors which are obsolescent at the time of publication of both magazines and books. These transistors are usually more expensive than equally suitable and readily available ones.

Stranded connecting wire, with pvc covering. It saves energy to have a variety of colours available.

Single-strand wire is useful for breadboard connections.

Screened wire is usually necessary for interconnecting equipment. Generally avoid the very thin, twin stereo cable, as this is easily broken.

Components are most readily connected together on copper-stripboard. Buy this in large pieces as it is very easily cut. Strips with holes 0.15″ distant will be found useful for general purposes, but integrated circuits will need 0.1″ pitch-holes. The copper strip may be broken with a few turns of a hand drill, and the most compact way of connecting can be worked out at first on graph paper.

Crocodile clips, both miniature and standard, are especially useful for temporary connections of batteries, variable resistors and plugs.

Standard jack-plugs and *Open jack-sockets* are good connections. The end of the plug is the signal connection and the screen (earth) is connected to the part above the insulating ring. There are, unfortunately, three different mouldings of the ends of these plugs available. The thin moulding may result in intermittent contact with some sockets. The type supplied by R.S. Components, 13–17 Epworth Street, London EC2P 2HA, seems to be the most satisfactory, but a similar moulding is made by other firms. DIN plugs and sockets are made with three and five connections. The five-connection variety are of two types. In one, the pins span an angle of 180 degrees and in the other, an angle of 270 degrees. The former is by far the most common (earth is the centre contact, numbered 2).

Much money and time can be wasted if an early decision on rationalizing connection is not made. Both DIN and Standard Jack connections will probably have to be used.

6 B.A. nuts, bolts and washers are the most useful for connecting sockets and so on to aluminium boxes.

Diagram 2

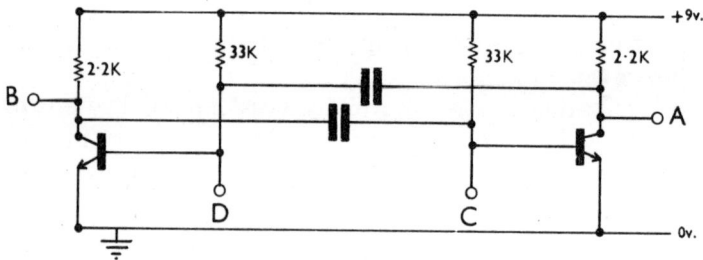

(d) Oscillators

Multivibrator. The example shown in Diagram 2 may be set up on an S-Dec in a few minutes. Output may be taken from any of the points A, B, C, or D (end of jack-plug) together with the common earth-line. Output from A or B will give a square-wave output (approx.). Evidence that the wave-shape decides the tone-quality will be heard by taking the output from points C or D, which give the approximate wave-shape
 . The substitution of resistance 3 or resistance 4 by a 100 k variable resistor will give a continuous range of frequencies.

Capacitor values: 0.01 – high audible range
0.1 – low audible range

Capacitors of 1 microfarad or more will give subsonic frequencies. These low frequencies may be used to effect automatic changes in a second multivibrator giving audio frequencies. The two circuits will need to be connected via a resistor (see Diagram 3).

Diagram 3

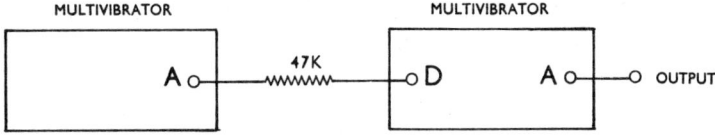

It will be heard that the pitch changes are not exactly two notes, indicating that the output of the control mutivibrator is not precisely a square wave. Considerable alterations in rhythm will result by using two capacitors of different values in the control multivibrator.

Experiment with other interconnections. A capacitor is normally inserted in the output line and a variable resistor, with the output connected to the centre and outer connections, joined to earth, and one of the points A, B, C, or D, will act as a volume control. An amplifier is not necessary to hear the sound of this circuit. The output will be quite audible, although lacking in bass, if any small loudspeaker such as a two-inch one from an old radio is connected across either 2.2K resistor.

Diagram 4

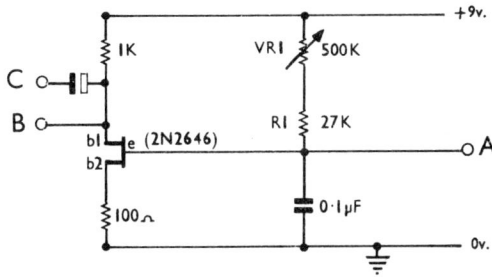

Unijunction Transistor Oscillator (see Diagram 4). This will produce three effective outputs: a ramp wave (/|/|/|) from point A, a pulse wave from point B (ᴧᴧᴧ) and a modification of the latter by a capacitor at point C. The audio range without change of capacitor is much greater than the multivibrator circuit described earlier. A second oscillator that could be made to control the first might have a 4.7 microfarad capacitor (C1), the output of which may be effectively taken from point A, via a 47K resistor, to point A, B or C of the audio oscillator. A triangle-wave output from point A may be obtained by removing VR 1, R 1 and C 1, and substituting the components shown in Diagram 5. The range will be limited to about a minor tenth.

Diagram 5

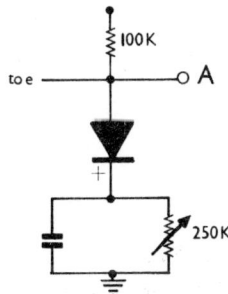

Square-wave Oscillator. The central component of this oscillator is a 741 operational amplifier (Diagram 6). Diagram 7 shows the pin connections as seen from above. It will be necessary to break the copper strips to isolate pin 1 from pin 8, and so on. With a one microfarad capacitor almost the whole audio range is available in one sweep. An oscilloscope shows the output from point A to be a good square-wave and that from point B to be a good triangle-wave in the higher register. These shapes become more distorted in the lower frequencies, and while a larger capacitor will preserve the shape to a lower frequency, the range of sound will be reduced in the upper register. VR 1 controls the pitch. Wave-shape, and hence tone-quality, may be varied with VR 2, but this also affects the pitch. Control wave-forms may be applied at point B through a variable resistor.

Diagram 6 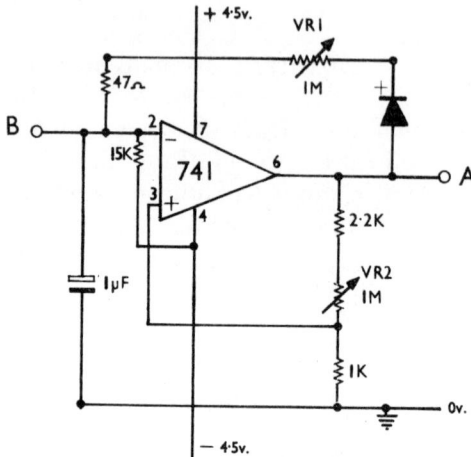   Diagram 7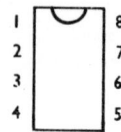

Square-wave oscillators may also be made from the logic integrated circuit 7400 N (FJH 131); these are very cheap and easily obtainable. An example is given in the article 'Wide Band Signal Injector' (*Practical Electronics*, April 1972), giving a fixed frequency which could be made variable by adding a variable resistor in series with one of the diodes or by placing a 1 k variable resistor between pin 14 and the positive power terminal. This was found to be suitable with a 4.5 V supply. The circuit may be constructed on a one-square-inch board.

Sine-wave oscillator. There are many versions available of the Wien Bridge circuit, for example, *Transistor Audio and Radio Circuits*, obtainable from Mullard (p. 178). This is suitable for an audio range, the stabilizing thermistor being the largest item of expenditure.

Transistor Radio. Without in any way impairing its normal function, any transistor radio may be converted to an amplifier or an oscillator with the addition of three soldered wires and a capacitor (see *Scientific American*, January 1973; 'Amateur Scientist' section).

Bass Sounds. The serious lack of bass sounds in our schoolrooms can be at least partly overcome by the construction and use of a number of individually boxed oscillators that are chromatically tuned to bass frequencies. The quality should be good if all are linked through a filter unit (possibly variable) which is connected to an amplifier, with good speakers. Each oscillator can be equipped with a fine tuning control, an on/off push-button, and a volume control. If the push-button is replaced by a key mechanism, the units can also be arranged under the control of one player. Separate, battery-powered oscillators, with 2½" speakers in the individual cases, will give poorer quality but will have the advantage of greater portability, a capacity for mechanical vibrato (by covering and uncovering the loudspeaker with the hand) and mechanical filtering (by placing cardboard, plastic containers and tubes over the loudspeaker), which will provide added interest to the exploration of sound.

Diagram 8

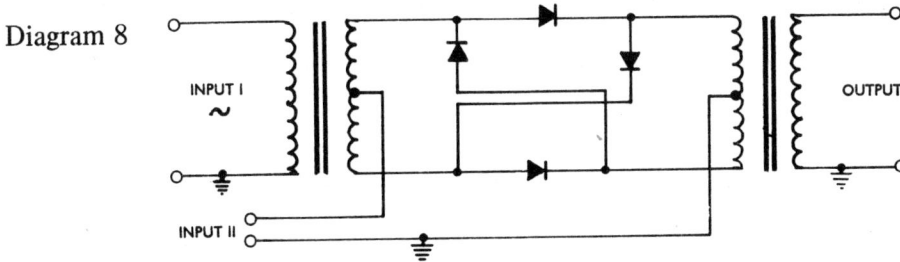

(e) A ring-modulator

The circuit shown in Diagram 8 employs any small, centre-tapped, one-to-one ratio transformer and four of almost any germanium diodes (packets of very cheap, unmarked diodes have been found to work well, but one must expect a few useless items in such a pack). The ring-modulator adds together the frequencies of inputs I (normally a sine wave) and II (another oscillator or any microphone input if a high impedance microphone is used); it also subtracts them. Unexpected chords are therefore produced if the sine-wave input is an audio frequency, and a tremolo effect is produced if the sine-wave input is from approximately 1 to 8 herz. The 'Dr Who' effects are rather typical of this by-now overworked device. The output level of the sine-wave oscillator will have to be continually adjusted as its frequency changes, to minimize distortion, which will in any case be considerably greater than that obtained from the more complex ring-modulators used in synthesizers.

(f) White noise

A good, variable-band, white-noise generator is of complex construction. Various effects may be obtained, however, by searching the frequency bands of a radio set, as may indeed a variety of other effects. Tapes of white noise, divided into separate one-octave and ⅓-octave bands, can also be purchased (from Tutchings Electronics Ltd, 14 Rook Hill Road, Christchurch, Hants).

(g) Other simple equipment

The following circuits described in the journals listed are all inexpensive, easy to make and work reasonably well:

Simple Fuzz Box — *Everyday Electronics*, December 1971
Waa Waa Unit — *Practical Electronics*, July 1970
Tremolo Unit — *Practical Electronics*, March 1972
Treble Booster — *Practical Electronics*, April 1972
I.C. Audio Mixer — *Practical Electronics*, January 1972
Hi-Fi Transistor Microphone — *Practical Electronics*, November 1968 (a microphone using a small crystal insert: this circuit is also a useful preamplifier for contact microphones and guitar pick-ups).

Musical Stave – *Practical Electronics*, May 1970 (sound is made when a metal pointer touches contacts arranged on five lines and four spaces).

Electronic piano – *Practical Electronics*, September 1972 et seq.

Synthesizer – *Practical Electronics*, February 1973 et seq.

(h) Simple rhythmic devices

Frequency-divider integrated circuits, in conjunction with a square-wave input with a positive peak of approximately 2.4 V to 4.5 V, provide four outputs which can be harnessed to a light display to give rhythmic patterns. They may also be used to control the frequencies of other oscillators. The speed of the patterns may be varied by altering the frequency of the square-wave input. Three of these dividers are available cheaply.

1. *Divide-by-sixteen counter* (SN7493)

The normal supply voltage is 5 V, but a 4.5 battery is satisfactory. The integrated circuit, which may be soldered on to 0.1 inch pitch veroboard, is shown here with the necessary connections (as seen from above):

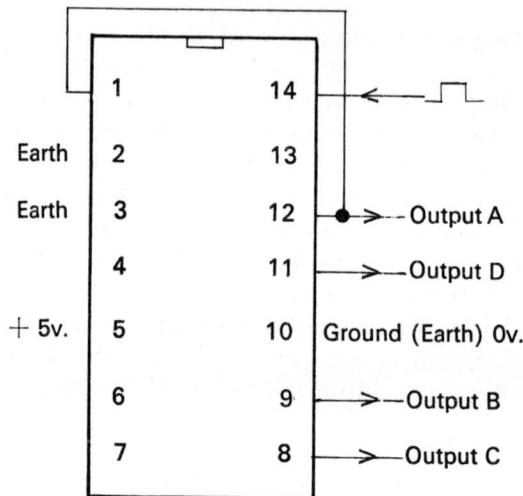

	1	14	← ⊓
Earth	2	13	
Earth	3	12	→ -- Output A
	4	11	→ — Output D
+ 5v.	5	10	Ground (Earth) 0v.
	6	9	→ — Output B
	7	8	→ — Output C

The connection of the lamps is shown below. The value of the resistor, typically 15 K, may need to be altered for individual transistors to obtain equal brilliance of lamps:

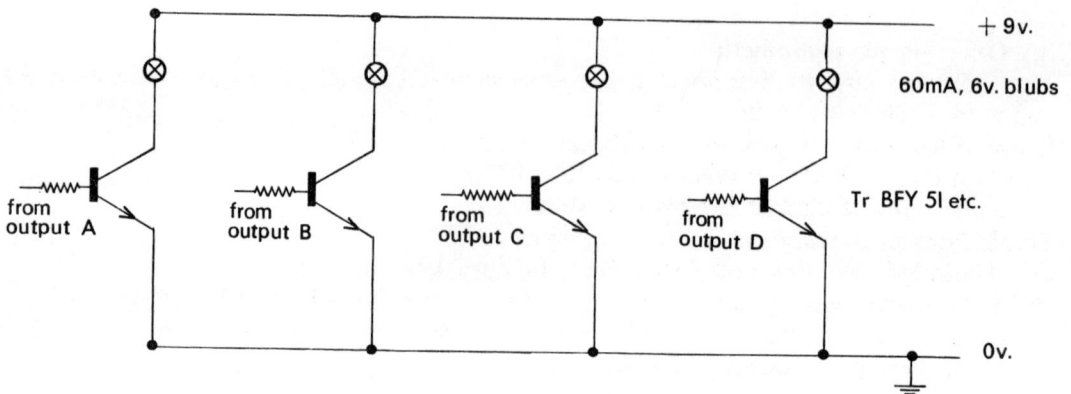

from output A   from output B   from output C   from output D

+ 9v.
60mA, 6v. blubs
Tr BFY 5l etc.
0v.

82

The truth table (1 = lamp on, 0 = lamp off) is:

D	C	B	A
0	0	0	0
0	0	0	1
0	0	1	0
0	0	1	1
0	1	0	0
0	1	0	1
0	1	1	0
0	1	1	1
1	0	0	0
1	0	0	1
1	0	1	0
1	0	1	1
1	1	0	0
1	1	0	1
1	1	1	0
1	1	1	1

Converting to musical notation, we have:

2. *Divide by twelve counter* (SN 7492)
Circuit connections:

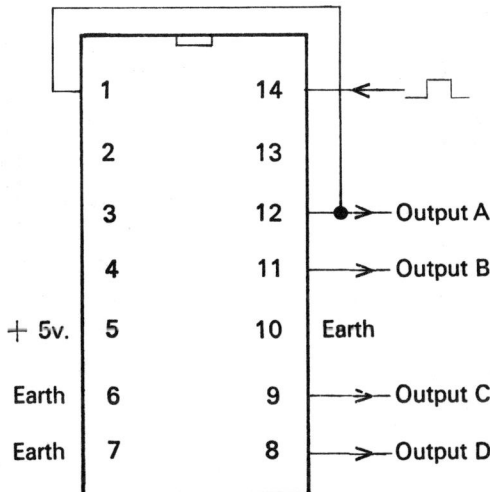

Musical notation for outputs:

A ... **B** $\frac{3}{2}$ ... **C** ... **D** ...

3. *Divide by ten counter*
First connecting method:

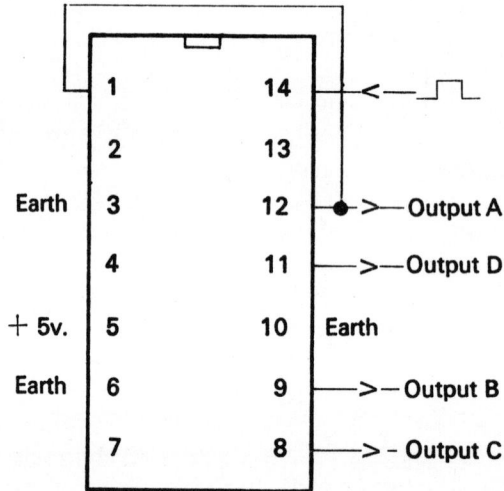

```
        ┌──────────────────┐
        │  1          14    │──< ─┌─┐─
        │                   │
        │  2          13    │
  Earth │  3          12    │──●>—Output A
        │  4          11    │──>—Output D
 + 5v.  │  5          10    │  Earth
  Earth │  6           9    │──>—Output B
        │  7           8    │──>- Output C
        └──────────────────┘
```

Musical notation for outputs:

A ... **B** $\frac{5}{2}$ ... **C** ... **D** ...

Second connecting method:

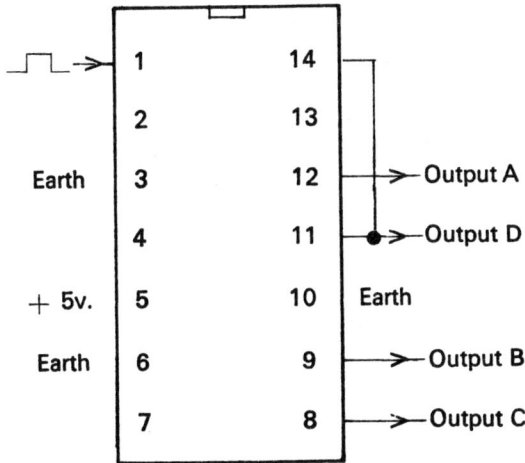

```
            ┌──────────────────────┐
  ⊓→        │ 1              14 ────┼─────┐
            │ 2              13     │     │
  Earth     │ 3              12 ────┼──►── Output A
            │ 4              11 ──●─┼──►── Output D
  + 5v.     │ 5              10   Earth
  Earth     │ 6               9 ────┼──►── Output B
            │ 7               8 ────┼──►── Output C
            └──────────────────────┘
```

Musical notation for outputs:

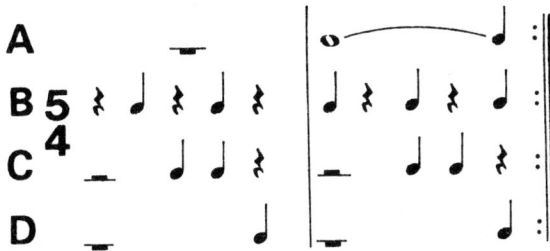

A SIMPLE STUDIO

The basic requirements are two tape-recorders and an amplifier. It will be preferable if these are stereo, thus incorporating two independent channels of sound-source. The addition of a record-player will be an advantage, but unless the items are to be transported from place to place, the purchase of instruments that have their own speakers and amplifiers will be unwise. To obtain a higher-quality amplifier and better speakers to serve all units, will prove more economical.

These are minimal requirements for a secondary school or a college of education, and the products of such equipment should result from an imaginative use of its limitations. It would be pointless to attempt to ape the products of institutions that possess computerized synthesizers, 24-track tape-recorders, and other sophisticated resources.

(a) Tape-recorders

Four-track machines enable one to store twice as much material as on a two-track. A two-track stereo machine is particularly useful if you wish to play recorded material backwards. If you have one two-track and one four-track you will have to remember to erase material recorded on the two-track machine before recording on the four-track, unless you wish to make use of this unorthodox method of 'superimposition'. Both machines should have two speeds, and preferably three. It is possible to modify a Revox A77 machine to play back at a continuously variable speed as well as its two fixed speeds. This is a useful modification, and it is worth while consulting an electronics engineer about the feasibility and cost of modifying one of your own machines. It is more comfortable to work with machines which can operate in the vertical position. There are great advantages in having machines which have separate erase, record and playback heads, together with separate preamplifiers for record and playback. While recording with such equipment, one may listen simultaneously to the quality of the recording, thus making it unnecessary to wind back and check afterwards. It also becomes possible to transfer a recording from one track to another, while at the same time adding a second recording, perfectly synchronized with the first.

Tape heads should be cleaned regularly. It is quite possible for a machine to be in otherwise perfect order but with recording rendered impossible because particles of dirt are keeping the tape away from the recording head.

(b) Connections

Apparatus will need to be connected (possibly using home-made and borrowed equipment as well as the fixed studio equipment) in a variety of ways. Nothing is more frustrating than continually having to connect and disconnect leads, and the effort and expense required to make a patchboard for the interconnection of apparatus, with wires permanently cleated to a work bench, is well worth while.

(c) Power

The amplifier and tape-recorders should be connected by 13 amp plugs (3 amp fuses are sufficient) to a block of sockets (possibly floating). The block of sockets is then connected to the mains. The record-player should be arranged to obtain its power from the amplifier where possible.

Diagram 9

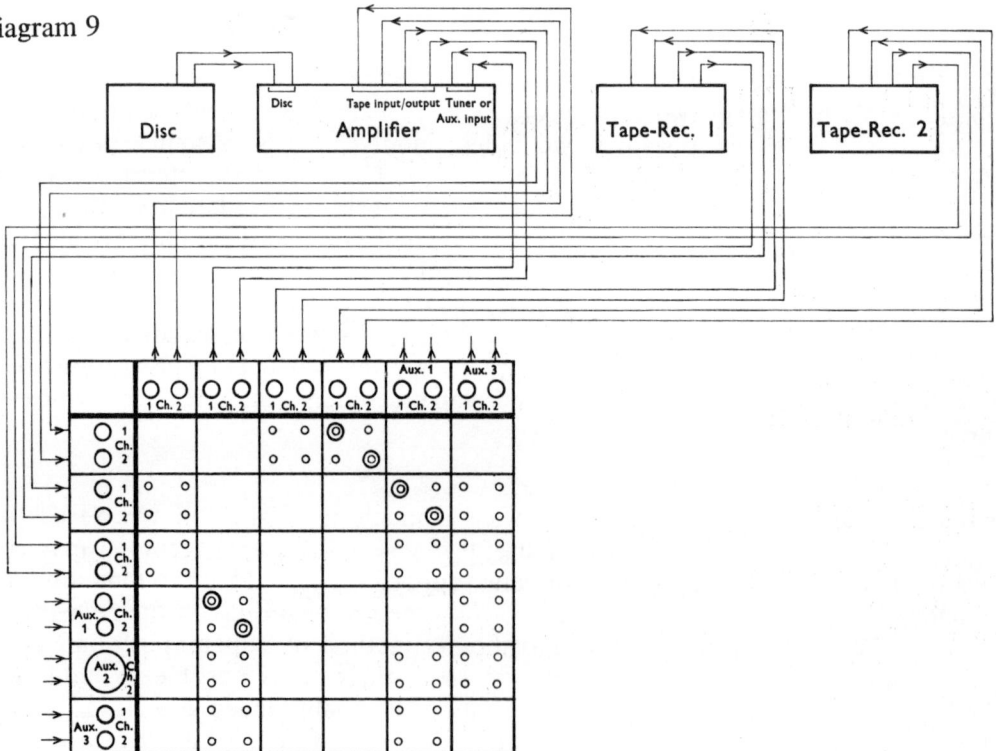

(d) Signal connections

Interconnections via a patchboard are shown in Diagram 9. All interconnecting leads should be screened, and as short as possible, to avoid loss of bass and general signal strength. These are joined to the aluminium patchboard (not drawn to scale) by jack-plugs. Signals FROM equipment go to the left side of the board. Signals TO the equipment go to the top of the board. Extra sockets have been added to make it possible to link other equipment. A DIN socket has been included for emergencies. The apparatus is interconnected by inserting a suitable plug into the appropriate miniature socket. The screen lines are connected to the aluminium box. The signal-input lines are connected to all miniature sockets in the same horizontal row at an unearthed contact. The signal-output lines are connected to all miniature sockets in the same vertical row at the second unearthed contact of the socket. As an example of the use of the patchboard, the sockets which are ringed show the sequence. Tape one output into Auxiliary 1 (perhaps a small synthesizer); the output of the synthesizer is then taken to the amplifier, and the signal finally recorded on tape-recorder two.

Microphones would be connected through a mixer, or directly to the apparatus concerned.

A PHOTORESISTOR CIRCUIT

Here is an example of the type of circuit mentioned at the beginning of this chapter. For knob control the photoresistors could be replaced by 1 or 2 megohm variable resistors. In Diagram 10 photocells 1 and 2 vary the frequencies of the oscillators, while 3 and 4 give emphasis to different harmonics in the filters. The two oscillator frequencies are mixed in a difference-amplifier to give three frequencies, the third being the difference between those of the two inputs. The output of the difference-amplifier is taken to a small power-amplifier. In this case a circuit built round a Sinclair IC 12 was used, with connection to an R.S. Components 6-inch Long Throw Speaker.

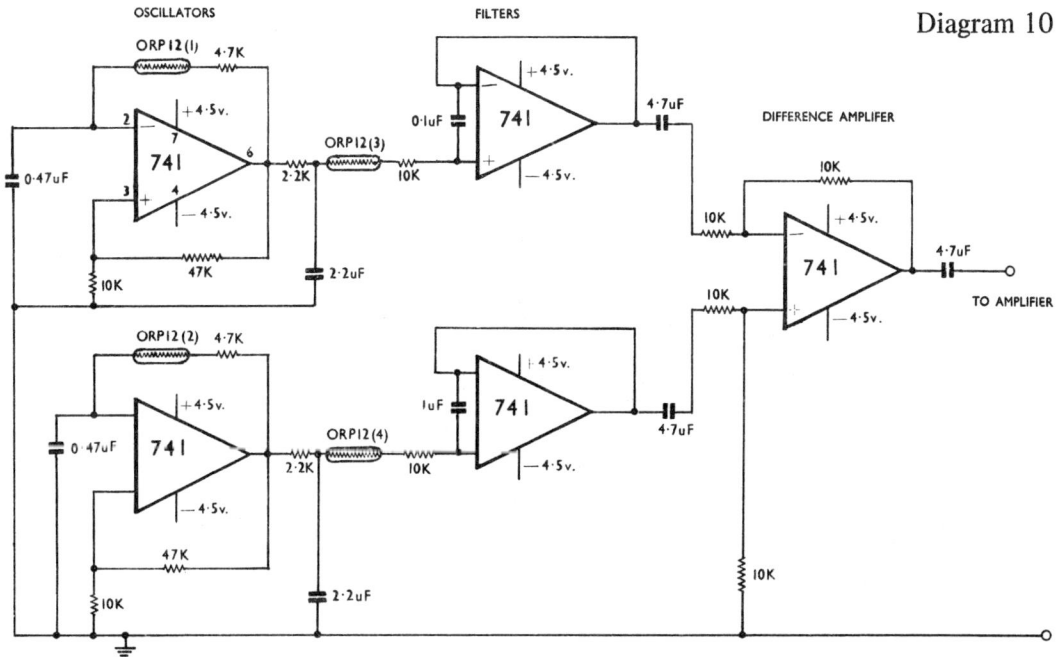

Diagram 10

87

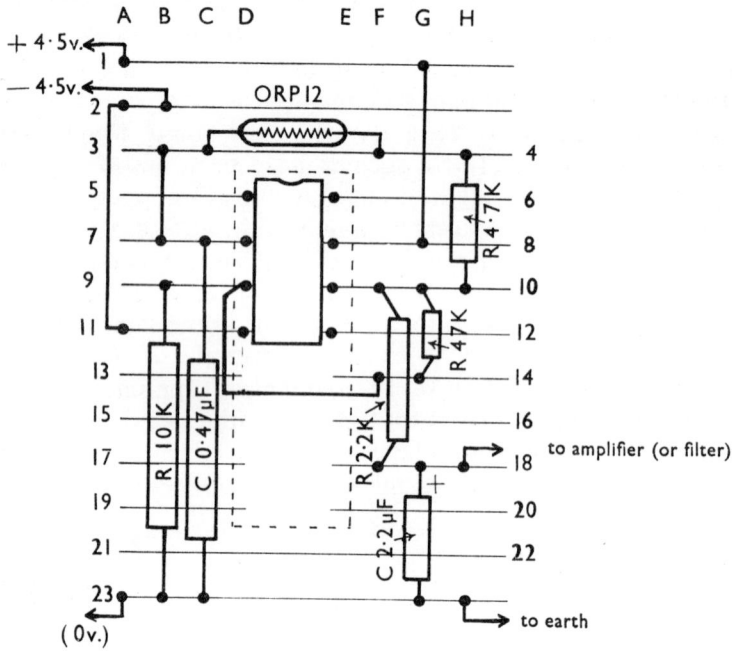

Diagram 11a

A B C D   E F G H

+ 4·5v.
1
− 4·5v.
2
ORP12
3   4
5   6
7   8
R 4·7K
9   10
11   12
R 47K
13   14
15   16
R 22K
17   18 to amplifier (or filter)
19   20
R 10K   C 0·47µF   C 2·2µF
21   22
23
(0v.)   to earth

Diagram 11b

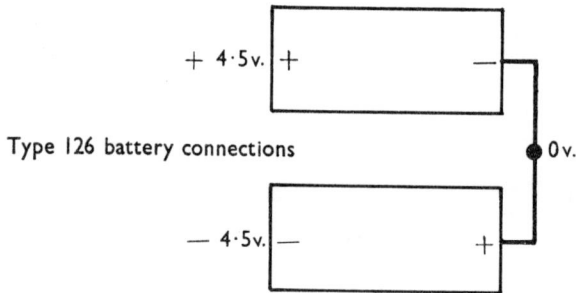

+ 4·5v. +   −

Type 126 battery connections   0v.

− 4·5v. −   +

Diagram 11c

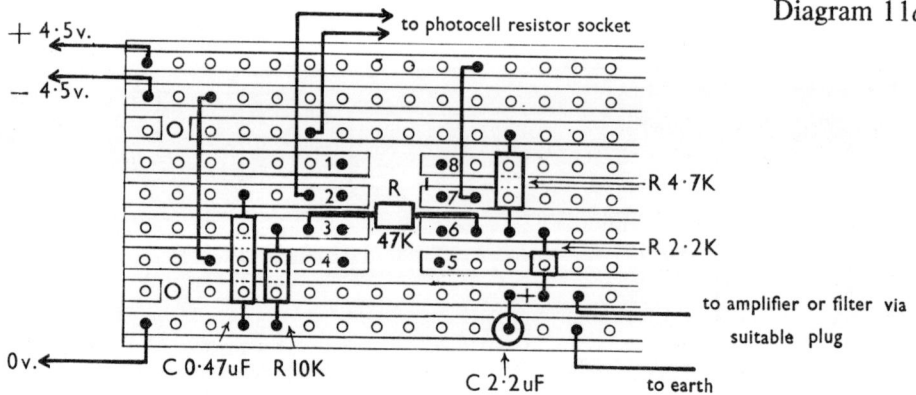

+ 4·5v.   to photocell resistor socket
− 4·5v.
                                    R 4·7K
                          R
                          47K   R 2·2K
                                    to amplifier or filter via
                                    suitable plug
0v.   C 0·47uF R 10K
                          C 2·2uF   to earth

88

In the dark there is no oscillation. By altering the angle and distance of a torch-beam in relation to the cells considerable variety of sound is obtainable.

The 2.2 K resistors and the 2.2 μF capacitors were introduced to convert the harsh square-wave into an approximate triangle-wave.

Diagram 11a shows a test set-up for one of the oscillators. Filters and a difference-amplifier could be set up by the same method. A μ-Dec is used. The dotted lines indicate an integrated-circuit adapter and 16-pin socket into which an 8-pin 741 integrated circuit is mounted. Continuous thin horizontal lines indicate permanent connections on the Dec. Various wire links have been added, with components inserted as follows:

Photocell	B3 – B7
0.4 μF	C7 – C23
10 K	B9 – B23
47 K	G10 – G14
2.2 K	F10 – F18
2.2 μF	G18 – G23

Diagram 11b shows battery connections.
Diagram 11c shows permanent connections on a piece of 0.1 pitch veroboard (enlarged).

> 1 – 8 – integrated-circuit pin connections
> small circles – holes in copper strips
> large dots – solder connections
> large circles – copper strip cut away (a few turns of a hand drill
>   with ⅛ -inch bit).

THE SYNTHESIZER

A small synthesizer, such as the VCS3, is not unreasonably priced, but one has to be thoroughly convinced of its value in comparison with, say, the same sum spent on orchestral instruments or on an electronic organ. With the cost equal to that of, perhaps, a good trumpet and a good bassoon, the synthesizer would in general be a better buy for a school because:
1. With due care it may be used by many people of different abilities (instead of perhaps one good performer, as with the bassoon):
   (a) for musical experiment and composition;
   (b) for dramatic purposes;
   (c) for wave-form demonstrations in conjunction with an oscilloscope.
2. It can effectively modify the tone of cheap electronic instruments (organ, stylophone, etc.) and vary the quality of all orchestral instruments.
   The patchboard (Diagram 9) is ready to accommodate a synthesizer at auxiliary one sockets – assuming that the synthesizer has no more than two inputs and outputs.
   I have found that College of Education students need to approach the problem of using the synthesizer as a composing instrument in two ways in parallel:
   (a) systematic working with each unit and its controls, singly and in various sequences;

(*b*) setting up pre-existing patches, reasoning out flow-diagrams of these, followed by modifications of dial settings, and removal and addition of pins, with careful observation of the results.

Diagram 12

VCS3 DOPE SHEET - *ELECTRONIC MUSIC STUDIOS (LONDON) LIMITED*

28

PROJECT /NAME /DATE	SHEET No :
PERFORMANCE / RECORDING NOTES	PATCH No :
	SETTING No :
	START TIME:
	END TIME :
	PERIPHERALS

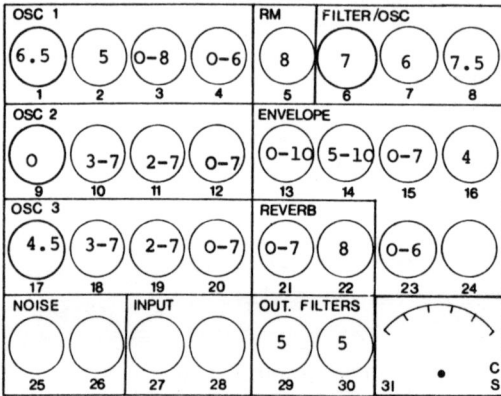

OSC 1 6.5 5 0-8 0-6   **RM** 8 **FILTER /OSC** 7 6 7.5
1 2 3 4   5 6 7 8

OSC 2 0 3-7 2-7 0-7   **ENVELOPE** 0-10 5-10 0-7 4
9 10 11 12   13 14 15 16

OSC 3 4.5 3-7 2-7 0-7   **REVERB** 0-7 8 0-6
17 18 19 20   21 22 23 24

NOISE 25 26   **INPUT** 27 28   **OUT. FILTERS** 5 5 29 30 31   C S

NUMBERS ARE DOPE SHEET REFERENCES, NOT PIN BOARD NUMBERS

CONTROL CHANGES
1—8
9—16
17—24
25—31
32—39

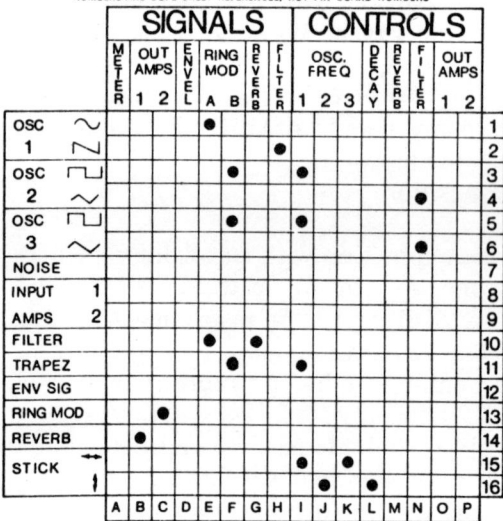

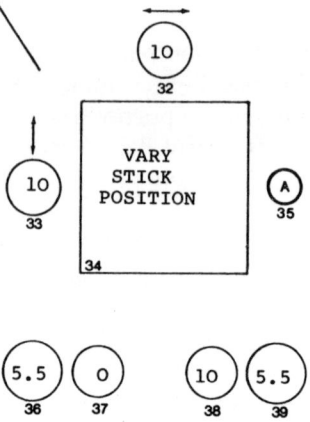

SIGNALS   CONTROLS

		METER	OUT AMPS 1	OUT AMPS 2	ENVEL	RING MOD A	RING MOD B	REVERB	FILTER	OSC. FREQ 1	OSC. FREQ 2	OSC. FREQ 3	DECAY	REVERB	FILTER	OUT AMPS 1	OUT AMPS 2	
OSC 1	∿					●												1
	∿							●										2
OSC 2	⊓⊔					●		●										3
	∿													●				4
OSC 3	⊓⊔					●		●										5
	∿													●				6
NOISE																		7
INPUT 1																		8
AMPS 2																		9
FILTER				●		●												10
TRAPEZ				●				●										11
ENV SIG																		12
RING MOD			●															13
REVERB		●																14
STICK	↔									●		●						15
	↕										●		●					16

A B C D E F G H I J K L M N O P

32

10

↕ 10 → 33

VARY STICK POSITION 34

(A) 35

5.5 0 10 5.5
36 37 38 39

90

Diagram 12 has been found effective for this purpose. It cannot be assumed that a student can necessarily see the potential of the possibilities, nor indeed can it be assumed that he will hear everything issuing from the loudspeaker.

While (*a*) is essential, (*b*) often provides a more effective stimulus, and makes the machine more widely available. Before such a course is complete students may be introduced to the use of the instrument as a modifier of tape input — in the form of instruments, voices, and noises. Tape compositions of reasonable quality, with or without live performance, can be expected using this method.

Perhaps the potentials of the synthesizer are better understood by the movement and drama students than by music students direct from the A-level syndrome.

POSTSCRIPT

Since this Section was written an abundance of information has become available on the construction of equipment suitable for electronic music.

Full details have been published on interesting small synthesizer designs by *Electronics Today, Practical Electronics* and *Wireless World.* A number of firms make the materials available as kits. One should be aware, however, that a kit does not necessarily include full construction information nor printed circuit boards.

The construction of electronic organs and pianos has been simplified by the availability of integrated circuits such as AY 1 − 0212, which, in conjunction with an oscillator and frequency dividers (for example, SN 7493) make available all necessary pitches with only one tuning control. See, for example, the article 'Electronic Piano Design' in *Wireless World,* May 1974.

Other useful special purpose i.c.s. include:

555 timer, used both as a monostable and astable multivibrator.

The low-noise preamplifier, LM 381.

The voltage-controlled oscillator 8033 (Intersil), with sine, square and triangle outputs.

Interesting extensions to small synthesizers giving programmed control may be made with t.t.l. and c.mos digital integrated circuits. It is a good idea to obtain databooks and handbooks on these families from one of the international corporations.

9. Miscellany

1. Fourteen exercises

These exercises are examples of types used in the 1960s to draw attention to single parameters. (I would now do much of this in a less formal way, and without notation.) An example might be a group improvisation using polystyrene pieces of various shapes and sizes on a highly polished floor. Something interesting always happens naturally to demonstrate anything musically important.

(1) Effect of density (number of attacks per time unit — here, 3–10 seconds)
(2) and (3) Attack
(4) Volume
(5) High, middle, low
(6) Intervals.
> NOTE: The following is a simple way of obtaining specific intervals by non-musicians on melodic percussion. Number each bar:

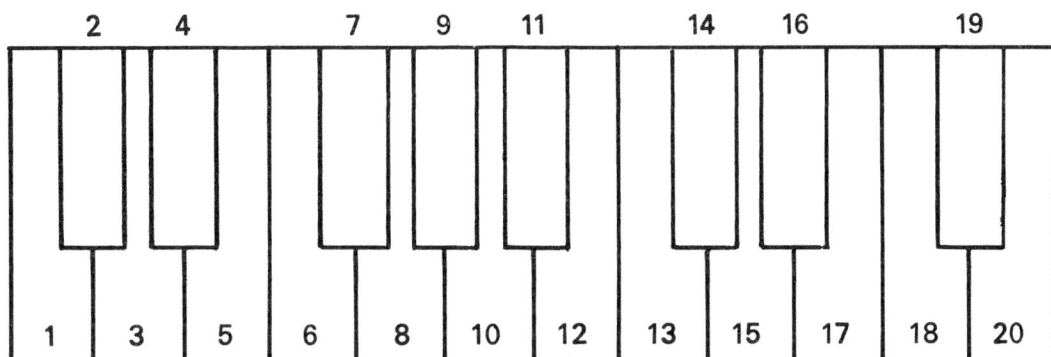

Give a formula for the desired interval; for example a minor third x + 3 . . . 1 + 4, 7 + 10, 12 + 15, etc.
(7) In (5), all instruments are used together in three registers. Here, in (7), these registers are part of the total pitch-registration ($\updownarrow$ denotes equivalence); for example, upper stave, glockenspiels; next stave, chime-bars; next, elementary violins; and so on, with the piano using any or all of the staves.
(8) The effect of a single chord of fixed registration.
(9) A performable doodle to complete the page.
(10) and (11) The effect of tone-colour distribution.
(12),(13),(14) Exercises where the information given is intended to be expanded in writing, with full and precise detail as to instrumentation, pitch, duration, attack, volume, etc.
(12) Given — density.
(13) Given — register.
(14) Given — volume.

Exercises 1–14

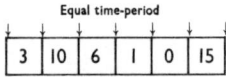

Exercise 1

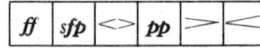

Exercise 4

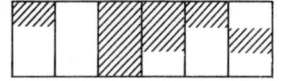

Exercise 5

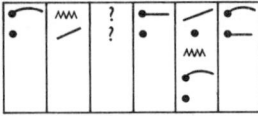

Exercise 3

Exercise 2

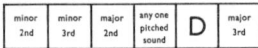

Exercise 6

Exercise 7

Exercise 8

Exercise 9

IMPROVISATION I

Exercise 10

IMPROVISATION II

Exercise 11

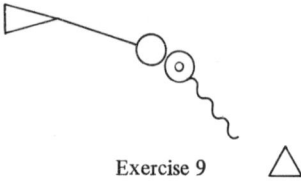

94

Exercise 12

Exercise 13

1			2		3	4				5	6		
0	5	10	15	2	25	3	35	4	45	5	55	0 5 10 15 20 25 30 35 40 45 50	

A

B

C

D

E

Exercise 14

2. Material for piece with audio-cueing

Each group is separately rehearsed. The teacher or leader has six instruments arranged so that they are not visible to the class.

In this example each group has its own cueing instrument. For example, Group A (each pupil has 3 xylophone bars) starts on the first cymbal sound, and ends on the second. Group C, cued by a tambourine, has two textures – playing texture 1 from Cue 1 to 2, and texture 2 from Cue 3 to 4. In texture 1 continuous repetition of their three pitches at a moderate speed, and in texture 2, a short tremolo, two rapid sounds, with a pause before each repetition of the texture.

Soft playing is necessary for the cues to be heard, the cue of course being sounds of the piece itself. Listening for the cues when several textures are heard together is a useful aid to intensive listening in performance.

A possible version is given. This has an interesting symmetry, but this in fact resulted from the use of a pack of playing cards. The succeeding example is a more elaborate working of the same idea.

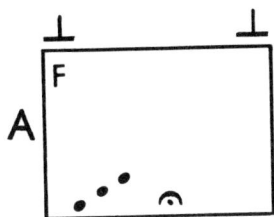

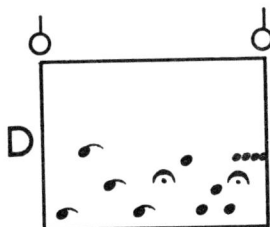

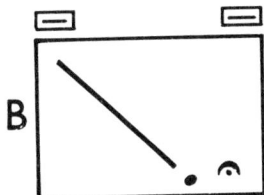

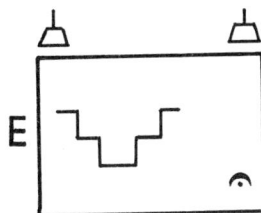

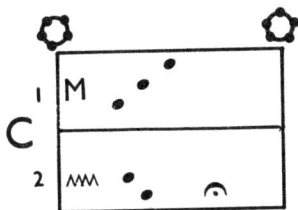

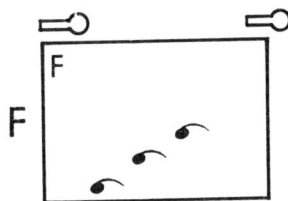

POSSIBLE VERSION

3. Improvisation material – for piano and percussion

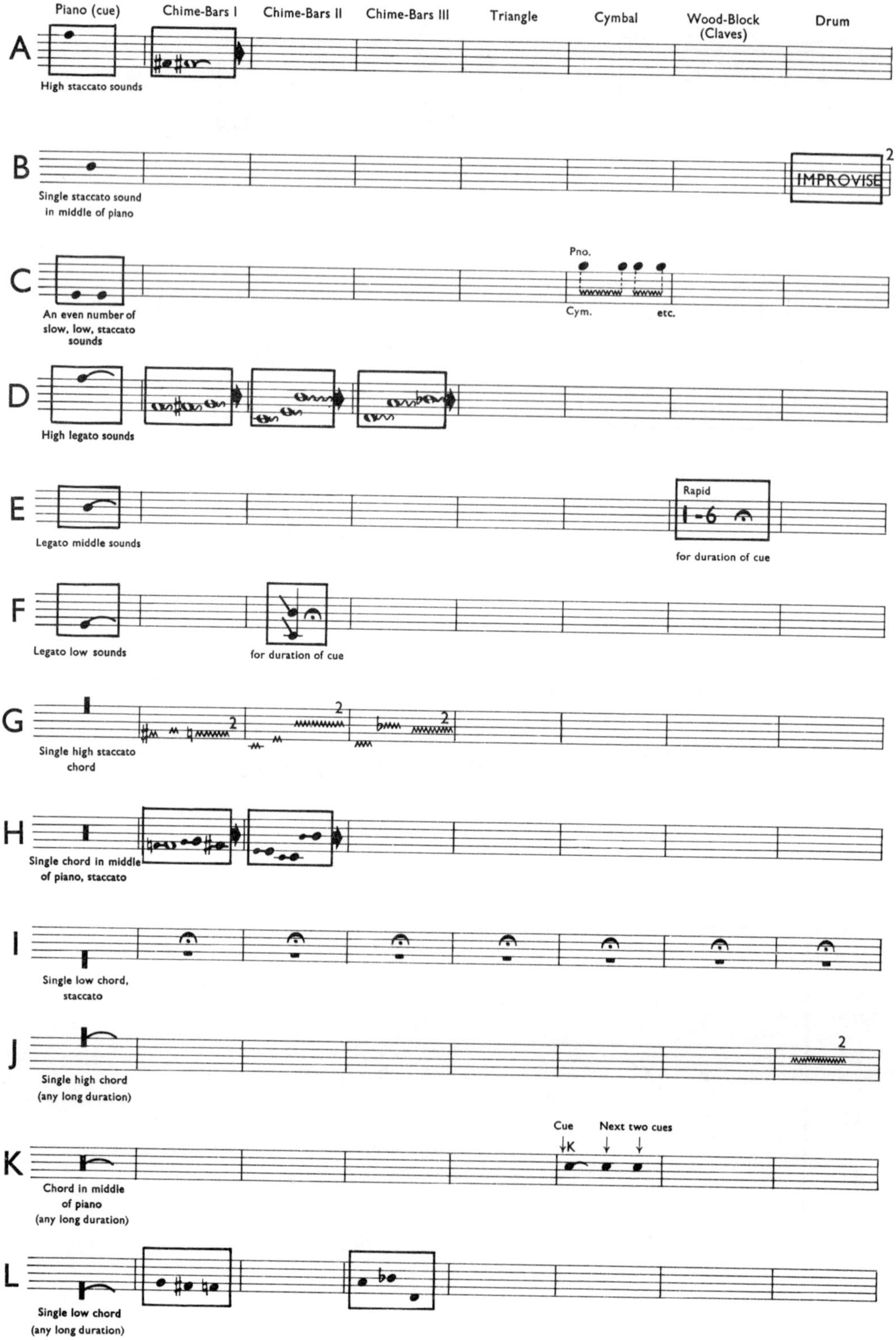

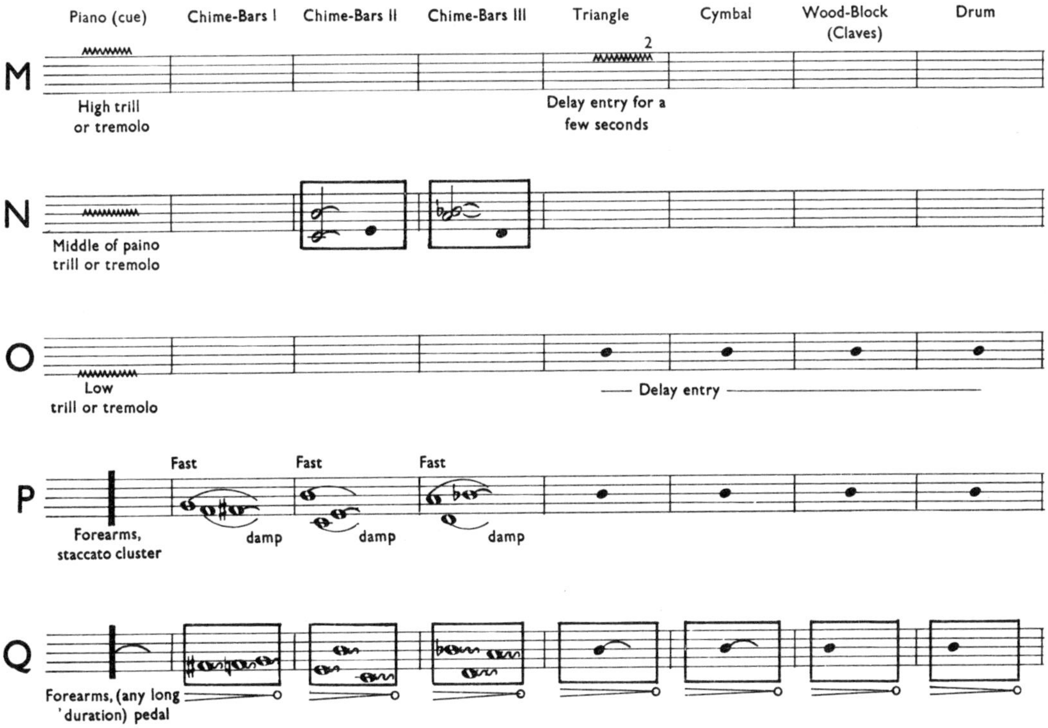
Piano (cue)
Chime-Bars I
Chime-Bars II
Chime-Bars III
Triangle
Cymbal
Wood-Block (Claves)
Drum
M
High trill or tremolo
2
Delay entry for a few seconds
N
Middle of paino trill or tremolo
O
Low trill or tremolo
Delay entry
P
Forearms, staccato cluster
Fast
damp
Fast
damp
Fast
damp
Q
Forearms, (any long 'duration) pedal

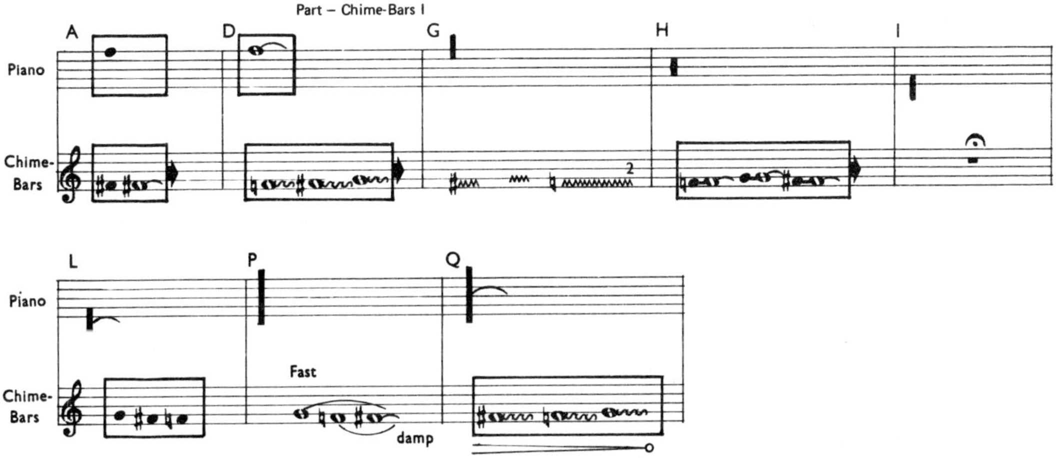
Part – Chime-Bars I
A
D
G
H
I
Piano
Chime-Bars
2
L
P
Q
Piano
Chime-Bars
Fast
damp

*The timing is up to each player, and these and similar attacks will only accidentally be simultaneous.

I (continued)

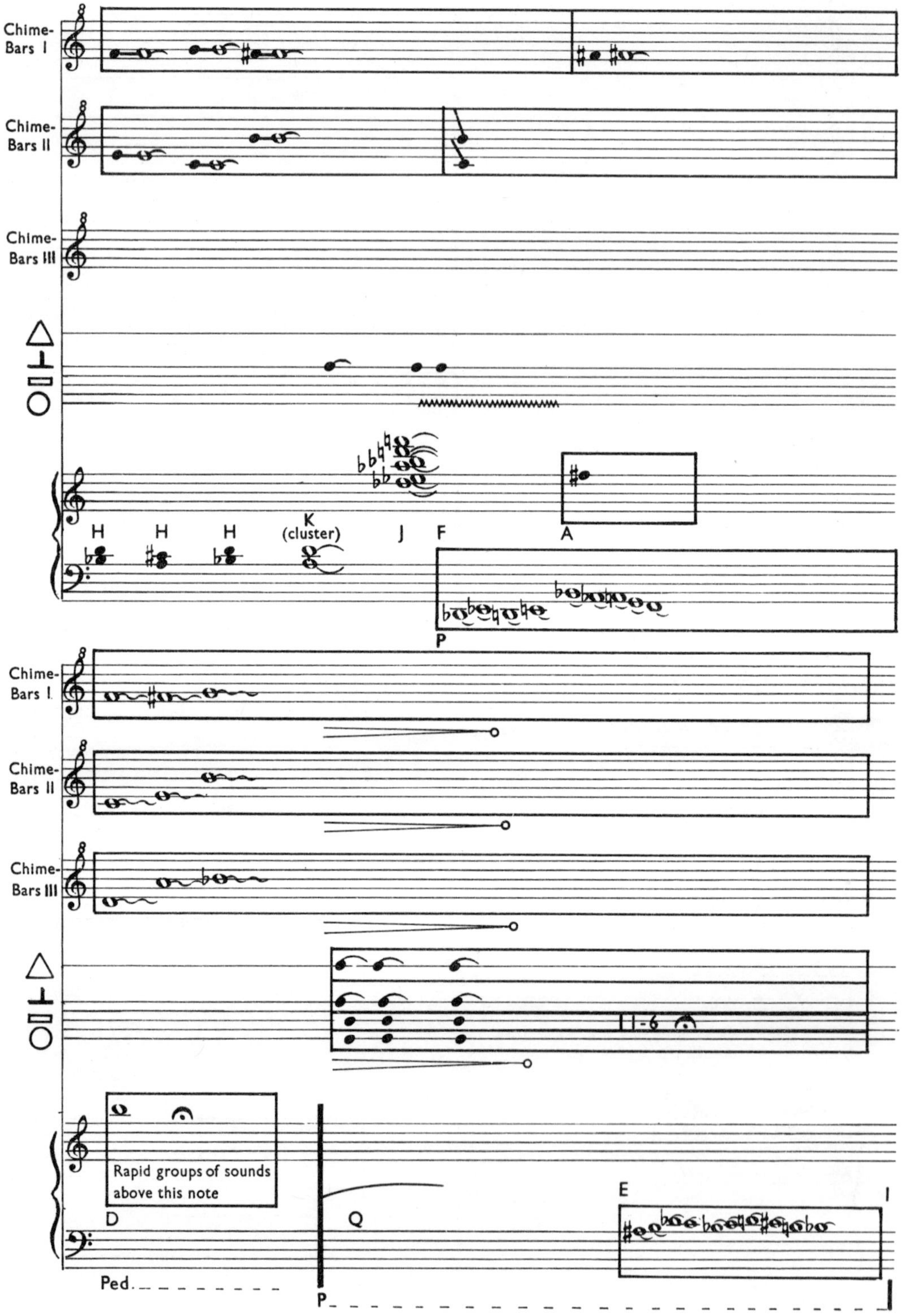
Chime-Bars I
Chime-Bars II
Chime-Bars III
H
H
H
K (cluster)
J
F
A
P
Chime-Bars I
Chime-Bars II
Chime-Bars III
11-6
Rapid groups of sounds above this note
D
Q
E
I
Ped.
P

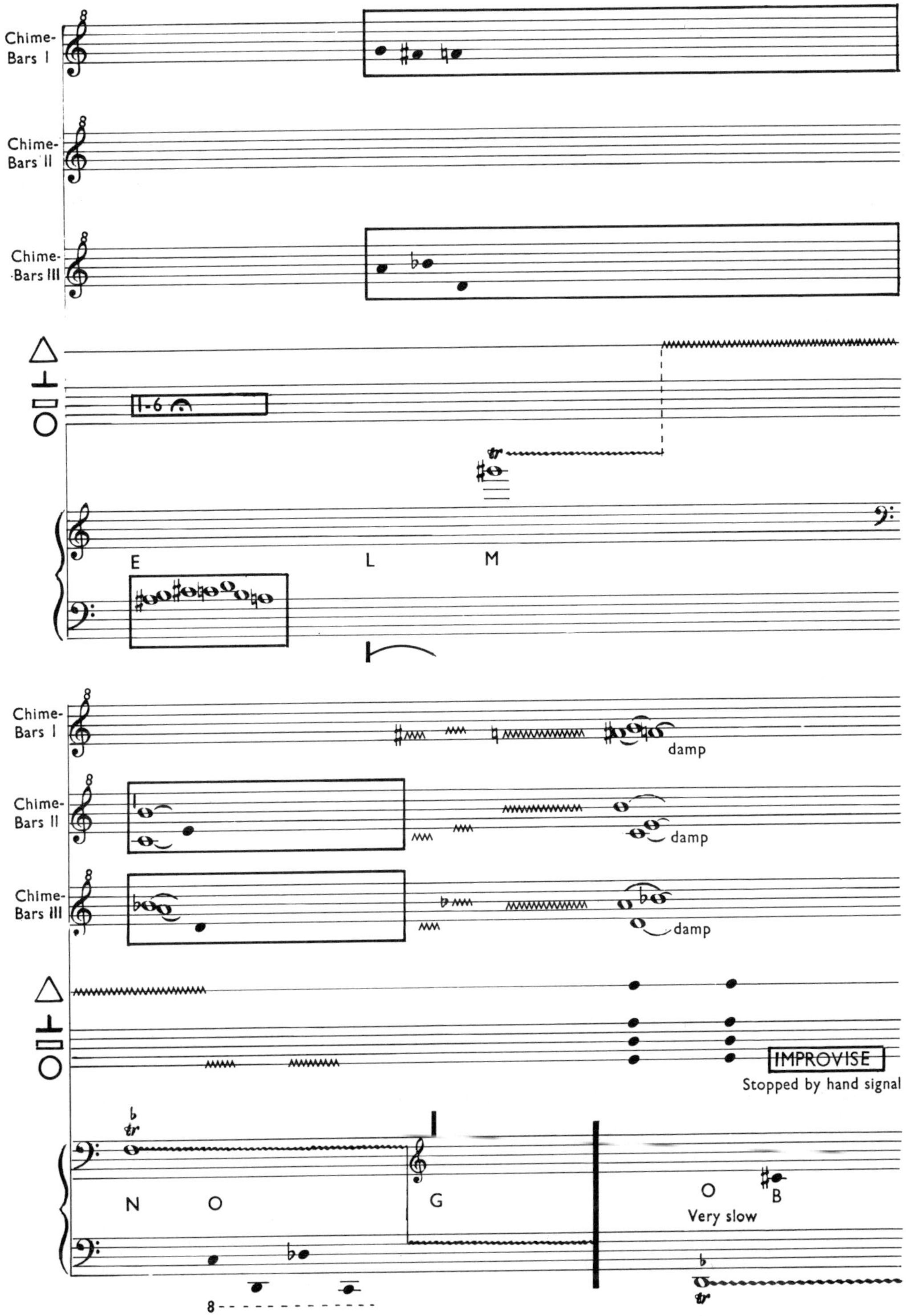
Chime-Bars I
Chime-Bars II
Chime-Bars III
11-6
E
L
M
Chime-Bars I
damp
Chime-Bars II
damp
Chime-Bars III
damp
IMPROVISE
Stopped by hand signal
N
O
G
O
B
Very slow
8

Before playing the two pieces arranged from the material, rehearse the players with each cue separately. Make other pieces by arranging the cues in any order. Changes in instrumentation may be made; there may be any number of players to each part (the piano material could be shared by two players).

PERCUSSION

repeat pattern, in varied rhythm, until the next cue is heard.

repeat until the next piano cue but one, unless the cues concerned give other instructions to the player.

start very loud and get softer gradually until another cue for the instrument is heard or until the sound of the instrument is no longer audible. Players play in the following rhythm — but individual players interpret beat duration:

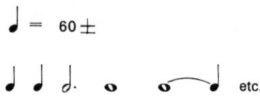

$$\downarrow = 60\pm$$

etc.

repeat pattern until another cue for the instrument is played.

short sound

sound which gradually dies away.

CHIME-BARS

strike, leaving head of beater on the bar, giving a dead staccato sound.

Use a strip of card with three holes, placing it between the resonator and the bars:

strike with hole closed, then open hole without restriking.

strike and cover and uncover hole continually while the sound lasts.

rub the edge of the metal bar with a triangle beater.

In Versions I and II timing of the events is controlled by the pianists; the volume generally results from listening among the players.

4. Make music with your name

Example:

• = I beat, — = 4 beats,

between letters = duration of previous letter

(between words = duration of previous word)

Alphabet	A	B	C	D	E	F	G	H	I	J	K	L
	Y Z	W X	V	U	T	S	R	Q	P	O	N	M
Code	A	B	C	D	E	F	G	F#	G#	B♭	C#	E♭

Example:

Combined rhythm - pitch examples:

5. Tour

Board diagram (numbers over letters in boxes):

Top row: `4/a` — `16/b` — `8/f` `24/o` — `8/o` `16/g` `16/o` `16/g` `16/o` `16/g` `16/o` `16/g` `8/o` — `8/o` — `2/e` `6/o`

Middle-left: `2/o` — `2/o` `4/a` `4/o` `4/a` `2/o`

Box: `3/c` `1/o`

Right: `32/o` ; `4/c` `4/o`

Legend:

a =	(14)
b =	(18)
c =	(9)
d =	(34)
e =	(18)
f =	(14)
g =	(70)
h =	(26)
o = silence	

Lower row (left): `16/o` `4/e` `4/f` `4/e` `4/h` `4/g` `4/h` `4/e` `4/h` `16/o`

Lower row (right): `8/o` `16/d` `16/o` `16/d` `8/o`

Bottom row: `4/o` `12/h` — `2/o` `2/a` `2/e` `4/o` `2/f` `2/b` `4/o` `2/c` `4/g` `2/o` `2/h` `2/d` `2/o`

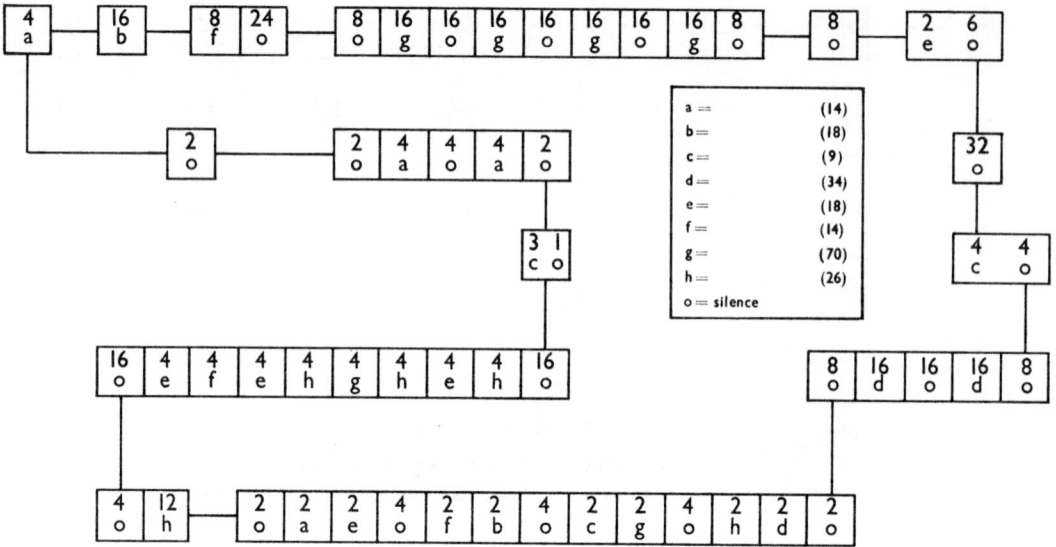

Start anywhere, and move clockwise or anti-clockwise. Use the whole route one or more times, or use only a part. Numbers in boxes indicate durations in any suitable time-unit. This unit may or may not be common to all performers. No breaks are intended between successive boxes, even if separated.

Each performer, using any sound source(s) he desires, completes the table in such a way that what is performed for one letter is different from that performed for all other letters.

The numbers in parentheses indicate the number of time-units devoted to each letter on one complete tour. Letter g has the most units and therefore should be the most monotonous, or alternatively, should be the most varied in its manner of performance.

Rules could be altered. For example, 'O' could designate something visual; silences could be freely used; time-units could be abandoned.

6. Musical Snakes and Ladders

The normal rules for snakes and ladders apply, except that dice are normally to be thrown by players in their own time and not in rotation, each performer having his own die. Individual cups should vary in size and material.

Sounds are not made when a 'six' is thrown. Sounds are made only at the top of ladders and the bottom of snakes. Sounds made are governed by the relevant pairs of figures.

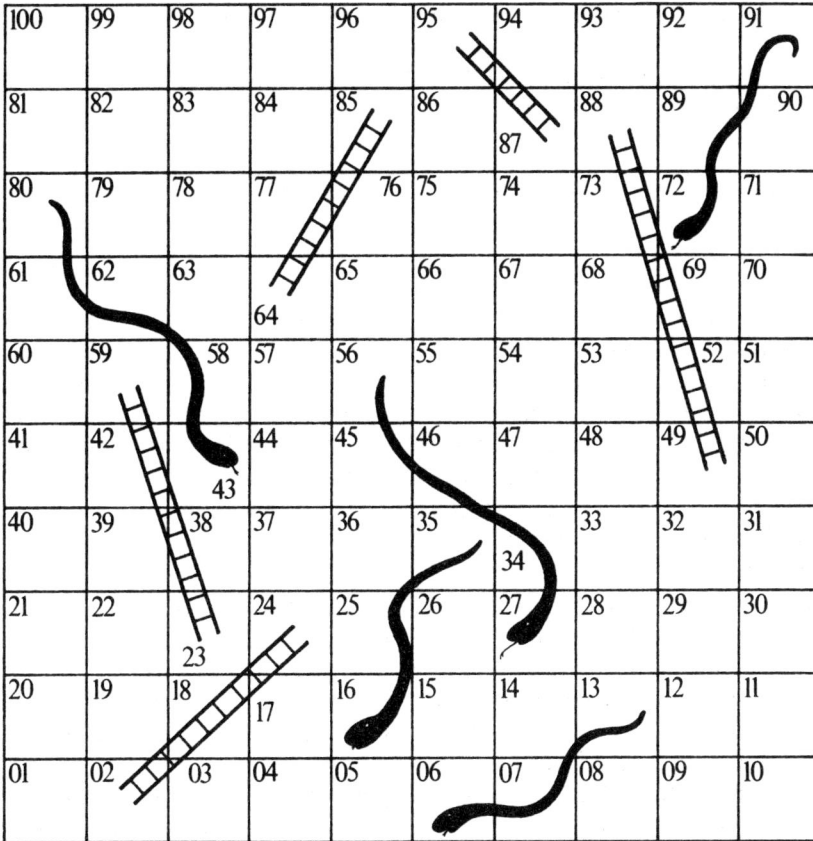

100	99	98	97	96	95	94	93	92	91
81	82	83	84	85	86	87	88	89	90
80	79	78	77	76	75	74	73	72	71
61	62	63	64	65	66	67	68	69	70
60	59	58	57	56	55	54	53	52	51
41	42	43	44	45	46	47	48	49	50
40	39	38	37	36	35	34	33	32	31
21	22	23	24	25	26	27	28	29	30
20	19	18	17	16	15	14	13	12	11
01	02	03	04	05	06	07	08	09	10

FIRST FIGURE

0 = Noise
1 = 1 pitch
2 = 2 pitches
.
.
.
9 = 9 pitches

SECOND FIGURE

gives duration
of the event
1 = 1 second
2 = 2 seconds
.
.
.
9 = 9 seconds
0 = 10 seconds

For '100', play the sound 'A' in sounds of maximum duration until all have played 'A' for a short time together. The die figure for each throw (1, 2, 3, 4, 5) may be used as a code for, say, volume, attack, duration of individual notes, and so on.

(Pitch possibly in conjunction with the name-game code)

A SPACE – TIME EXPERIENCE

NOTES ON PERFORMANCE

1. For performance by six groups, with about six performers in each group. There are no special qualifications required of performers.
2. Performance is normally in private, in a large hall or gymnasium. A performance may be video-taped for later playback to the performers. At least one camera should be positioned to view the whole area without changes (or with very infrequent changes) in focus and angle, and to record continuously. Other cameras may be used to focus on incidents. Playback should be from the

continuous recording, with other recordings on separate screens or inserted in the main tape.

3. The hall is divided into twelve areas. Area 1 is central, other areas are well separated and in any order.

4. *Materials:*
   (*a*) Eight lots of dowelling of many diameters (from ⅛″ to 1½″) and of many lengths (from about 3′6″ to 2″). These are compiled to provide diversity of length and/or diameter, and placed in areas 5–12.
   (*b*) Three lots of corrugated plastic tubing. In the first performance twenty-four 'whirl-a-tune' tubes were purchased, twelve of each of two colours. Eleven of each set of tubes were shortened, so that two chromatic octaves were available. The three lots then consisted of twelve tuned tubes of one colour (area 3), twelve tuned tubes of a second colour (area 4) and off-cuts from tubes of both colours (area 2). In this case, each colour of tubing had a different diameter. Other materials may be substituted for (*a*) and (*b*).
   (*c*) Footwear, which performers remove on entering the hall and place in area 1.
   (*d*) The objects referred to in 5(*b*).

5. Each area is marked by:
   (*a*) A large card which bears the number of the area, together with instructions for each of the six groups. (Each group visits each area once.)
   (*b*) An object on or near which the card is placed. The object should be varied: examples might be a table, a chair, a small platform, a signpost, a dismembered nude dummy, a wire cage, a trolley or folding clothes airer, and so on.

6. Duration – about 25 to 45 minutes.

7. It is not intended that this space–time experience be rehearsed in any way, but the following information should be given to the performers, possibly in an adjacent room, before starting.

INSTRUCTIONS TO PERFORMERS

(*a*) Each of twelve areas is clearly indicated by a numbered card. Each group visits each area once.

(*b*) On each card are independent instructions for groups A B C D E and F.
   Each instruction contains:
   (i) The words AUDIO, VISUAL or AUDIO-VISUAL.
   (ii) In some cases amplification of (i)
   (iii) 'On signal, go to/remain in Area . . . .'

(*c*) Only the given materials may be used in carrying out instructions *b*(i) and *b*(ii) above:
   AUDIO – make sounds with the given materials.
   VISUAL – make patterns with the given materials.
   AUDIO-VISUAL – make audio and visual patterns with the given materials simultaneously.
   If there is no amplification of these instructions, details are left to the ingenuity of the performers.

(*d*) At the beginning of each section a clear, audible signal is given (possibly on a gong). The timing of signals is decided by the organizer according to the average interest of activity in the room. Participants who are bored could inspect other activities until the next signal.

(*e*) On the first signal place your footwear in area 1 and then search the twelve area cards until you find the starting instructions for your own group; for example, area card 7 has 'Group C start here'.

The twelve area cards are reproduced on the following pages.

AREA 1

Group E	Group B
VISUAL	VISUAL
Each performer in the group makes his own pattern of shoes. Each pattern must link with at least one other.	Alter the scale of the existing pattern of shoes. Do this again and again. On signal do not move the shoes.
ON SIGNAL GO TO AREA 7	ON SIGNAL GO TO AREA 9
Group F	**Group C**
AUDIO	VISUAL
	The group form a pattern by the addition of all shoes one at a time. When complete, build the same pattern at a distant place in the room. Do this again and again. On signal leave the shoes where they are.
ON SIGNAL GO TO AREA 7	ON SIGNAL GO TO AREA 9
Group A	**Group D**
VISUAL	AUDIO
Each performer in the group makes his own pattern of shoes in a different area.	
ON SIGNAL GO TO AREA 10	ON SIGNAL GO TO AREA 2

Group D VISUAL Alter the patterns of other groups with your tubes. Take them back to AREA 2 before moving to your new area on signal. ON SIGNAL GO TO AREA 3	**Group A** AUDIO ON SIGNAL GO TO AREA 6
Group E AUDIO Make sounds appropriate to the silent movement in Area 4. Return the tubes to Area 2 before going to new area on signal. ON SIGNAL GO TO AREA 1	**Group B** AUDIO ON SIGNAL GO TO AREA 1
Group F AUDIO Set up strong rhythmic patterns as a group. ON SIGNAL GO TO AREA 12	**Group C** AUDIO Go individually to Area 5, Area 8, or Area 10. Aurally, disrupt or support activities there with your tubes as you consider appropriate. Return the tubes to area 10 before going to new area on signal. ON SIGNAL GO TO AREA 10

Group B AUDIO Do *not* whirl the tubes. Do *not* use the tubes as trumpets. ON SIGNAL GO TO AREA 8	**Group E** VISUAL Alter the patterns of other groups with your tubes. Take them back to Area 3 before moving to your new area on signal. ON SIGNAL GO TO AREA 4
Group C VISUAL Throw tubes to one another over big distances. Cease on signal, or when all tubes have fallen to the ground, whichever is the sooner. Leave the tubes where they have fallen. ON SIGNAL GO TO AREA 5	**Group F** AUDIO Twirl the tubes only; in some groups organization of sound. ON SIGNAL GO TO AREA 1
Group D VISUAL React with your tubes to each of the other groups in turn (without sound). Return the tubes to Area 3 before moving to new area on signal. ON SIGNAL GO TO AREA 10	**Group A** AUDIO Use the tubes only as trumpets. Announce your presence to each of the other groups in turn. ON SIGNAL GO TO AREA 9

Group B VISUAL Make silent patterns only, in the air. Move only within your own area. ON SIGNAL GO TO AREA 10	**Group F** VISUAL Alter the patterns of other groups with your tubes. Take them back to Area 4 before moving to your new area on signal. ON SIGNAL GO TO AREA 6
Group C AUDIO Do *not* whirl the tubes. Do *not* use the tubes as trumpets. ON SIGNAL GO TO AREA 1	**Group D** AUDIO Twirl the tubes only, moving at the same time over the whole hall. Return the tubes to Area 4 before going to next area on signal. ON SIGNAL GO TO AREA 12
Group E AUDIO Use the tubes as trumpets. React to other groups, display yourselves as soloists in prominent positions. Return the tubes to Area 4 before moving to new area on signal. ON SIGNAL GO TO AREA 5	**Group A** VISUAL Make silent patterns only, in the air. Move throughout the whole performing area. Return tubes to Area 4 before going to new area on signal. ON SIGNAL GO TO AREA 1

Group E AURAL ON SIGNAL GO TO AREA 6	**Group B** AUDIO ON SIGNAL GO TO AREA 3
Group F start here VISUAL Make a pattern by the addition of sticks singly until all are used. The pattern, to which all have contributed, should be satisfactory at each stage. If there is time inspect other patterns in the room. ON SIGNAL REMAIN IN AREA 5 AUDIO ON SIGNAL GO TO AREA 10	**Group C** AUDIO Make sounds independently. Go to another area for this, but return sticks to Area 12 before moving on signal. ON SIGNAL GO TO AREA 8
Group A AUDIO Tapping with the ends of two sticks on the ground, each member of the group establishes his own independent beat. After a while all members of the group attain a common beat. All groups then establish a common beat. This is maintained and decorated while groups move in one large circle anti-clockwise. ON SIGNAL VISUAL Each group forms its own circle of sticks and tubes on the ground. Get the sticks and tubes from anywhere. Each circle interlocks with at least one other. There should be no sticks or tubes which are not part of the circles. On completion, collect and put on own shoes, and leave the room without disturbing the patterns of sticks and tubes.	**Group D** AUDIO Make sound patterns only, in the air. Remain in your own area. ON SIGNAL GO TO AREA 6

Group A VISUAL The group forms a pattern by the addition of all sticks one at a time. When complete, build the same pattern at a distant place in the room. Do this again and again. Take the materials back to Area 6 before moving on signal to next area. ON SIGNAL GO TO AREA 7	**Group D** AUDIO Make sound patterns only, in the air. Use the whole performing area. ON SIGNAL GO TO AREA 7
Group B start here VISUAL Make a pattern by the addition of sticks singly until all are used. The pattern, to which all have contributed, should be satisfactory at each stage. If there is time, inspect other patterns in the room. ON SIGNAL REMAIN IN AREA 6 AURAL ON SIGNAL GO TO AREA 5	**Group E** AUDIO Make sound patterns only, in the air. Move only within your own area. ON SIGNAL GO TO AREA 2
Group C VISUAL As a group, form a pattern by the addition of all sticks one at a time. When complete alter the scale of the pattern. Do this again and again. ON SIGNAL GO TO AREA 4	**Group F** AUDIO ON SIGNAL GO TO AREA 3

Group F AUDIO Make sound patterns only, in the air. Move only within your own area. ON SIGNAL GO TO AREA 8	**Group C start here** VISUAL Make a pattern by the addition of sticks singly, until all are used. The pattern, to which all have contributed, should be satisfactory at each stage. If there is time inspect other patterns in the room. ON SIGNAL REMAIN IN AREA 7 AUDIO ON SIGNAL GO TO AREA 6
Group A VISUAL As a group, form a pattern by the addition of all sticks, one at a time. When this is complete, build the same pattern on a different scale at a distant place in the room. Do this again and again. Take the materials back to Area 7 before moving to the new area on signal. ON SIGNAL GO TO AREA 8	**Group D** VISUAL Make silent patterns. Pass sticks to one another. ON SIGNAL GO TO AREA 9
Group B AUDIO Tapping on the ground with the ends of two sticks, each member of the group establishes his own independent beat. After a while all members of the group attain a common beat. All groups then establish a common beat. This is maintained and decorated while groups move in one large circle anti-clockwise. ON SIGNAL VISUAL Each group forms its own circle of sticks and tubes on the ground. Get the sticks and tubes from anywhere. Each circle interlocks with at least one other. There should be no sticks or tubes which are not part of the circles. On completion, collect and put on your own shoes and leave the room without disturbing the patterns of sticks and tubes.	**Group E** AUDIO-VISUAL ON SIGNAL GO TO AREA 8

Group A AUDIO ON SIGNAL GO TO AREA 3	**Group D** VISUAL As a group, form a pattern by the addition of all sticks one at a time. When this is complete, alter the scale of the pattern. Do this again and again. ON SIGNAL GO TO AREA 1
Group B VISUAL As a group, form a pattern by the addition of all sticks one at a time. When complete, build the same pattern again at a distant place in the room. Do this again and again. Take the materials back to Area 8 before proceeding to the new area on the signal. ON SIGNAL GO TO AREA 2	**Group E** VISUAL Make silent patterns. Pass sticks to one another. ON SIGNAL GO TO AREA 11
Group C AUDIO Tapping on the ground with the ends of two sticks, each member of the group establishes his own independent beat. After a while all members of the group attain a common beat. All groups then establish a common beat. This is maintained and decorated while groups move in one large anti-clockwise circle. ON SIGNAL VISUAL Each group forms its own circle of sticks and tubes on the ground. Get the sticks and tubes from anywhere. Each circle interlocks with at least one other. There should be no sticks or tubes which are not part of the circles. On completion, collect and put on your own shoes and leave the room without disturbing the patterns of sticks and tubes.	**Group F** AUDIO-VISUAL Drop sticks for random patterns. Do this again and again. ON SIGNAL GO TO AREA 9

Group B AUDIO Fast, continuous, exciting rhythmic sound. ON SIGNAL GO TO AREA 4	**Group E** VISUAL As a group, form a pattern by the addition of all sticks one at a time. When this is complete, alter the scale of the pattern. Do this again and again. ON SIGNAL GO TO AREA 12
Group C AUDIO ON SIGNAL GO TO AREA 2	**Group F** VISUAL Make silent patterns in the air. Use the whole performing area. ON SIGNAL GO TO AREA 2
Group D AUDIO Tapping on the ground with the ends of two sticks, each member of the group establishes his own independent beat. After a while, all members of the group attain a common beat. All groups then establish a common beat. This is maintained and decorated while groups move in one large circle anti-clockwise. ON SIGNAL VISUAL Each group forms its own circle of sticks and tubes on the ground. Get the sticks and tubes from anywhere. Each circle interlocks with at least one other. There should be no sticks or tubes which are not part of the circles. On completion, collect and put on your own shoes, and leave the room without disturbing the patterns of sticks and tubes.	**Group A** AUDIO Make sound patterns only, in the air. Move only within your own area. ON SIGNAL GO TO AREA 4

Group A AUDIO-VISUAL Drop sticks for random patterns. Do this again and again. ON SIGNAL GO TO AREA 5	**Group C** AUDIO-VISUAL Drop sticks for random patterns. Do this again and again. ON SIGNAL GO TO AREA 11
Group B VISUAL Make silent patterns only, in the air. Make use of the whole performing area. Return sticks to Area 10, before going to new area on signal. ON SIGNAL GO TO AREA 11	**Group D** AUDIO ON SIGNAL GO TO AREA 4
Group F VISUAL As a group, form a pattern by the addition of all sticks one at a time. When complete, alter the scale of the pattern. Do this again and again. ON SIGNAL GO TO AREA 11	**Group E start here** VISUAL Make a pattern by the addition of sticks singly until all have been used. The pattern, to which all have contributed, should be satisfactory at each stage. If there is time inspect other patterns in the room. ON SIGNAL REMAIN IN AREA 10 AUDIO ON SIGNAL GO TO AREA 9

Group C AUDIO Make sound patterns only, in the air. Move within your own area only. ON SIGNAL GO TO AREA 12	**Group F** AUDIO ON SIGNAL GO TO AREA 4
Group D start here VISUAL Make a pattern by the addition of sticks singly until all are used. The pattern, to which all have contributed, should be satisfactory at each stage. If there is time, inspect other patterns in the room. ON SIGNAL REMAIN IN AREA 11 AUDIO ON SIGNAL GO TO AREA 8	**Group A** AUDIO ON SIGNAL GO TO AREA 2
Group E AUDIO Tapping on the ground with the ends of two sticks, each member of the group establishes his own independent beat. After a while, all members of the group attain a common beat. All groups then establish a common beat. This is maintained and decorated while groups move in one large circle, anti-clockwise. ON SIGNAL VISUAL Each group forms its own circle of sticks and tubes on the ground. Get the sticks and tubes from anywhere. Each circle interlocks with at least one other. There should be no sticks or tubes which are not part of the circles. On completion, collect and put on your own shoes and leave the room without disturbing the patterns of sticks and tubes.	**Group B** AUDIO-VISUAL ON SIGNAL GO TO AREA 12

Group D AUDIO-VISUAL Drop sticks for random patterns. Do this again and again. ON SIGNAL GO TO AREA 5	Group A start here VISUAL Make a pattern by the addition of sticks singly until all are used. The pattern, to which all have contributed, should be satisfactory at each stage. If there is time, inspect other patterns in the room. ON SIGNAL REMAIN IN AREA 12 AUDIO ON SIGNAL GO TO AREA 11
Group E AUDIO ON SIGNAL GO TO AREA 3	Group B AUDIO Make sounds independently. Go to another area for this, but return sticks to Area 12 before moving on signal. ON SIGNAL GO TO AREA 7
Group F AUDIO Tapping on the ground with the ends of two sticks, each member of the group establishes his own independent beat. After a while all members of the group attain a common beat. All groups then establish a common beat. This is maintained and decorated while groups move in one large circle anti-clockwise. ON SIGNAL VISUAL Each group forms its own circle of sticks and tubes on the ground. Get the sticks and tubes from anywhere. Each circle interlocks with at least one other. There should be no sticks or tubes which are not part of the circles. On completion, collect and put on your own shoes and leave the room without disturbing the patterns of sticks and tubes.	Group C AUDIO Make sound patterns only, in the air. Make use of the whole performing area. Return sticks to Area 12 before moving to new area on signal. ON SIGNAL GO TO AREA 3

10. More new sounds

I have been frequently asked by those who have worked through *New Sounds in Class*, 'Where do we go from here?' The answer of course varies according to who the pupils are, who the teacher is, and when the situation arises.

The six examples here provided give some possible answers.

More new sounds — 1

Directions for performance

Designed for a chromatic octave of chime-bars, but numerous combinations possible.

either initial attack with rubber beater with continuous rubbing of edge of chime-bar with metal beater *or* tremolo with two beaters.

undamped sound.

damped immediately after attack.

At *b* and *c* play as rapidly as is practical; make 'a short but distinct pause.

indicates repeat as necessary until the signal concerned.

Spacing is not indicative of timing, which is free and could often be regular.

GEORGE SELF

(a) e.g. 6 six rapid unpitched sounds

(b) *staccato*, the beater not to rebound

(c) damp at each pause

(d) different volumes and attacks (solos) (*p-ff*)

More new sounds — 2

Directions for performance

This piece is written for glockenspiels (parts 1, 2, 3) the chime-bars and/or metallo-phones (parts 4, 5, 6). It may however be adapted to include the use of xylophones, pianos, autoharps, guitars, etc. Registers may be altered. For example, parts 1, 2, and 3 may be sounded one octave lower than written. There may be any number of players to each part.

The piece is written with the idea of the learning of pitch notation in mind. Each player must perform:
1. On D
2. On one other pitch ⎤ noted exactly
3. On a small chromatic range — the range only indicated (e.g. part 1 uses B, C, C#, D, E♭, E).

(*a*) ┣━━▶ improvise, making use of all pitches within the given range

(*b*) ○━━▶ repeated note

(*c*) ◢━━▶ upward *glissandi*; alternately on black and white notes, or according to the structure of the instrument, within the given range

(*d*) ◥━━▶ downward *glissandi* in a similar way

(*e*) ● damped immediately after attack

(*f*) ᕦ◠ undamped sound

(*g*) ᕦ⇃ damp the sound after a longer period of vibration than ●

The time-interval between signals, which need not be constant, is at the discretion of the conductor. The speed of the sounds in (*a*), (*b*), (*c*), and (*d*) should normally be fast.

1 2 3 4 5 6
15 15 15 8 8 8
1 2 3 4 5 6 7 8 9 10 11 12 13 14 15
pp ppp pp ppp pp
pp pp pp pp
pp pp pp
pp pp pp
pp pp pp pp
pp ppp pp ppp
16 17 18 19 20 21 22 23 24 25 26 27 28 29 30
mp p ff mf pp
mp p ff pp
mp p ff pp f
mp p ff pp
mp p ff pp mp
mp pp p ff pp

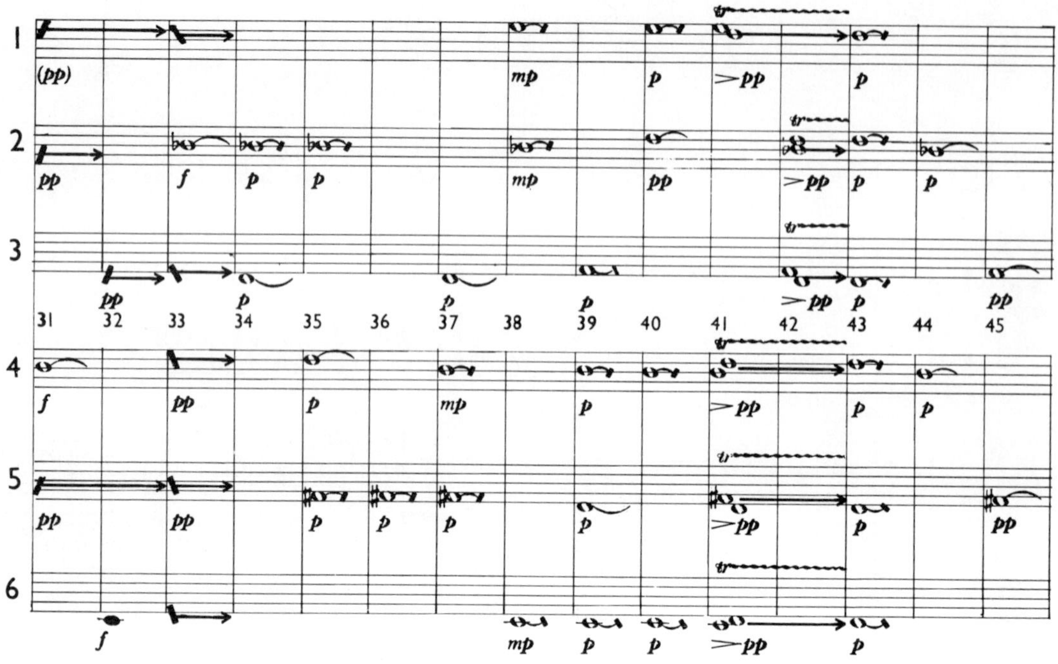

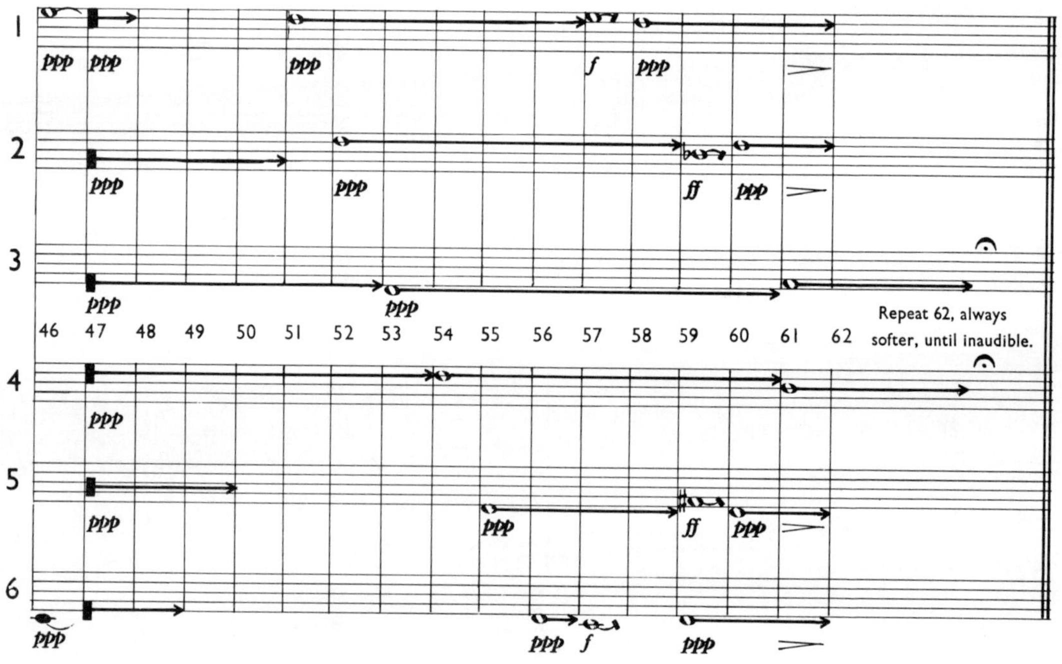
Repeat 62, always softer, until inaudible.

More new sounds — 3

Directions for performance

Staves A, B, C, D. Three pitches for each stave:

Flats or sharps occur only on the first appearance of a note

Stave E: one performer, with three staccato instruments, untuned, e.g. wood-blocks, small drums, or a mixture of instruments.

Stave F: one to three performers, with three resonant instruments, probably untuned e.g. cymbals, gongs. Piano clusters in three registers could be substituted.

STAVES A, B, C, D: probably one performer to each of the twelve pitches; playing chime-bars, or any mixed ensemble. Perhaps adapt for a smaller number of performers. Maybe reorchestrate to give individual players more than one pitch (draw rings around the pitches to be played).

 single sound of precise duration. Where durations cannot be achieved (perhaps in bars 41—45), repeated notes should not be introduced.

 trill or tremolo
damped immediately after attack
undamped sound

This piece is intended to be rather quiet and very precise throughout. Varieties of attack may be introduced as desired.

MORE NEW SOUNDS — 3   GEORGE SELF

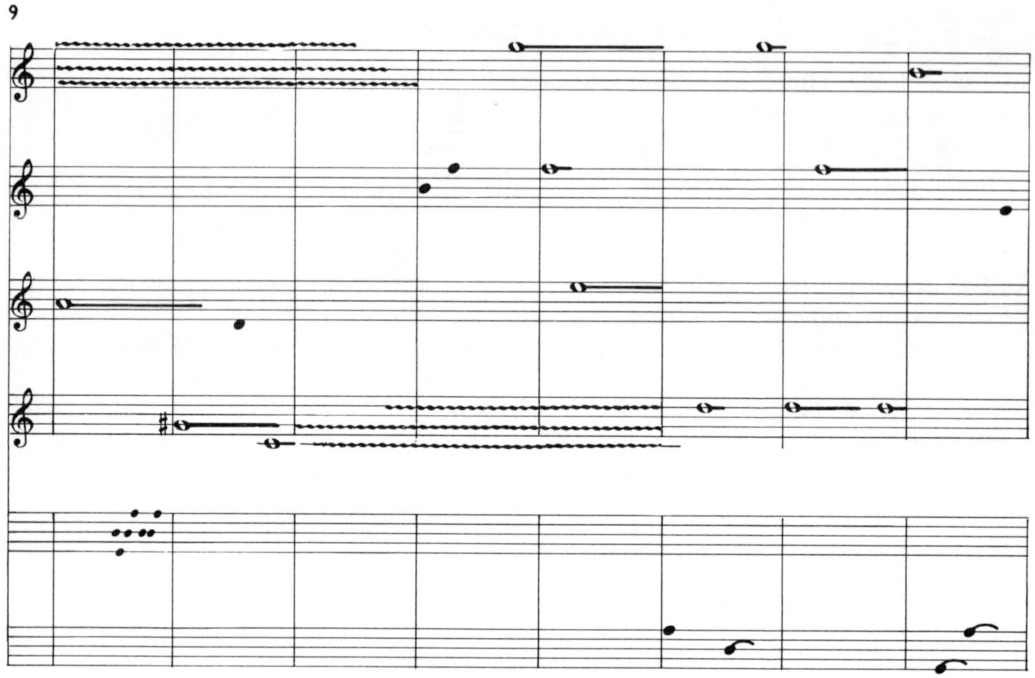
9

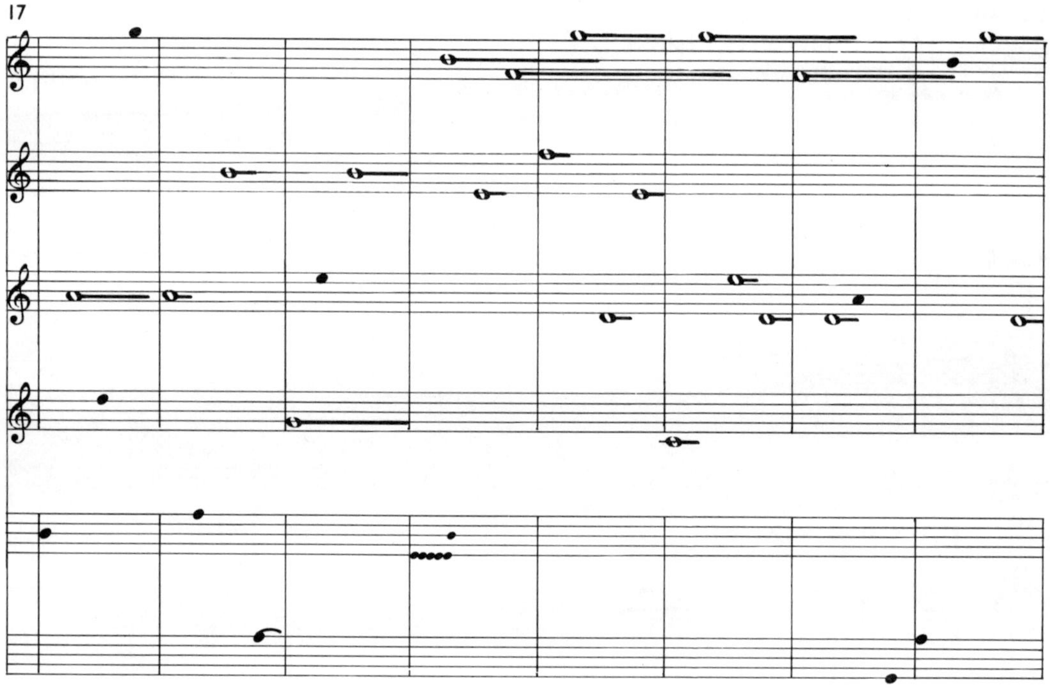
17

A little faster

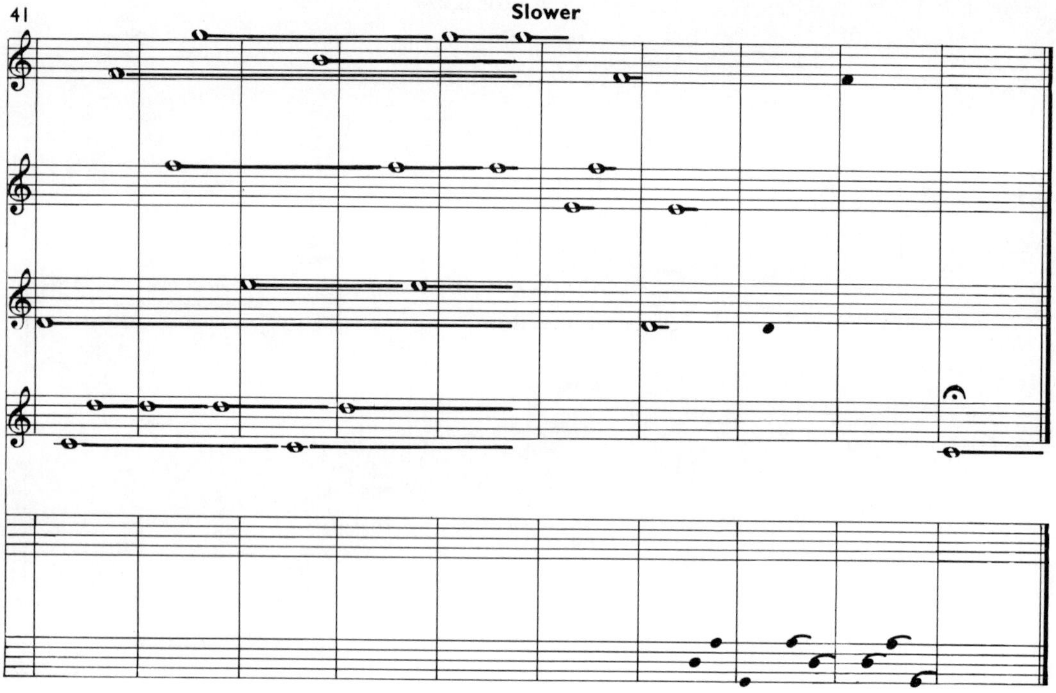
41
Slower

More new sounds — 4

GEORGE SELF

Gong

Cymbals

felt stick

4
5 ff

1 - 5
Slow taps around the rim, metal sticks
pp

1 - 3
Single high sounds of maximum length separated by 5-second silences pp

Melodicas

4
5
6
low f

Pianos

1a
1b
2a
2b

1b
ff

Pedal down, sweep strings slowly and softly

Gong
Wood Stick f

Cymbals

1
2
3
Drag metal stick from centre to rim several times mf

4
5
Drag metal stick from centre to rim several times mf

Melodicas

1 - 3

1
2
3
4
5
6
Low trills, rather slow pp

1
2
3
4
5
6
High Clusters
pp pp pp pp pp pp

Pianos

1a f

2a Quietly sweep strings—pedal down

1a
1b
2a
2b
Rapid random hand clusters ff, no pedal fast

2a
2b
Slow, short sounds Pluck p

Gong
Wood ff

Cymbals

1
2
3
4
5
Near Rim — — — gradually — — — to centre
Metal sticks
Slow, short sounds
ppp

Centre felt stick long sounds
pp

Wood Sticks
fff

1
2
3
4
5

Melodicas

1 - 6
Slow
ppp

1 H pp
2 M pp
3 L pp
4 M pp
5 L pp
6 M pp

H ff

Pianos

1a Slow, no pedal
1b ppp

2a
2b Slow Pluck pedal ppp

ff

ff

ff
fff

Gong

36 37
Slow, let ring, felt stick

pppp

Melodicas

Performers stop individually as they run out of breath

clusters

Spacing does not neccssarily indicate relative timing.

Volume contrasts are intended to be quite violent.

Pianos

Pedal down as keys are released, until no sound

36 37

131

More new sounds — 5

VEITCH DIAGRAM PIECE

GEORGE SELF

			AI = 4		AI = 1	
					A2 = 7-1	
1		**2**		**3**	A3 = 4 **4**	
		C2 = 2		C2 = 5		
		C3 = 4				
	BI = 1-7	BI = 5	AI = 1-7		AI = 5	BI = 7-1
	B2 = 3	B2 = 7-1	A2 = 2	B2 = 1-7	A2 = 1-7	B2 = 2
5	B3=7-1	**6**		**7**	A3 = 7-1 **8**	B3=5
		CI = 7-1		CI = 1		
		C2 = 3				
		C3 = 6		C3 = 1		
	BI = 2	BI = 3				
					A2 = 4	B2 = 5
9	B3=1-7	**10**	A3 = 1-7	B3 = 1 **11**	**12**	B3=3
	DI = 7-1	DI = 1-7	CI = 4	DI = 3		
	D2=7-1		C2 = 7-1	D2 = 2		
D3 = 1	D3 = 1-7	C2 = 1-7	D3 = 5	C3 = 7-1		
					AI = 7-1	
			A2 = 5			
13		**14**	A3 = 6 **15**		A3 = 2 **16**	
	DI = 5	CI = 1-7	DI = 2	CI = 5		
D2 = 1-7		C2 = 1-7	D2 = 6		D2 = 3	
			D3 = 7-1		D3 = 3	

The conductor decides the order of events, and may or may not decide upon the speed of a common beat.

Each event may be of any length; events may occur more than once.

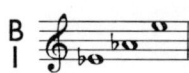

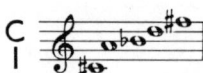

A1 B1 C1 D1 — Untuned percussion one instrument

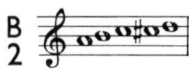

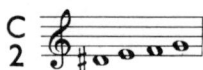

A2 B2 C2 D2 — Untuned percussion two instruments

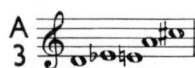

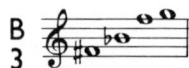

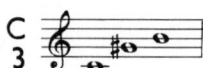

A3 B3 C3 D3 — Untuned percussion three instruments

1/2/3/4/5/6 = number of beats duration for sounds

1 - 7 — Number of beats duration varying according to the series 1,2,3,4,5,6,7.
7 - 1 — Number of beats duration varying according to the series 7,6,5,4,3,2,1.
Pitch succession (instrument seccession in D2 and D3) decided by performers.

132

PART C

Player C1

Player C2

Player C3

Example:
C2 – Square 6

Example:
C3 Square 11

	①	②	③	④
Player C1				
Player C2		2	5	
Player C3		4		

	⑤	⑥	⑦	⑧
C1		7 - 1	1	
C2		3		
C3		6	1	

	⑨	⑩	⑪	⑫
C1			4	
C2		1 - 7	7 - 1	
C3			7 - 1	

	⑬	⑭	⑮	⑯
C1		1 - 7	5	
C2		1 - 7		
C3				

PART D

Player D1 — one untuned percussion instrument

Player D2 — two untuned percussion instruments

Player D3 — three untuned percussion instruments

D1

D2

D3

Example:
D1 Square 11

Example:
D3 - Square 11

	⑨	⑩	⑪	⑫
D1		7 - 1	1 - 7	3
D2		7 - 1		2
D3	1	1 - 7	5	

	⑬	⑭	⑮	⑯
D1		5	2	
D2	1 - 7		6	3
D3			7 - 1	3

More new sounds — 6

This is intended as a class piece without the conductor making specific aural-training points.

1. It gives vocal evidence of following a score.
2. The student learns the sound of a minor third and attempts to sing this against interference.
3. The student needs to recognize two sounds in unison.

    (In the initial recording it was found impossible to obtain a unison with the apparatus available, a difference-tone varying between 1 and 2 per second being present. This was mostly not heard, and its recognition was an extra bonus of the exercise).

TAPE In the original performance, limited materials were available. Each part of the texture was separately recorded. With the aid of a stop-watch and blank tape these were then collected together (superimposed as necessary), the timing depending partly on the interest of the texture, partly on the estimated 'reaction' time required for a class.

variously banded-noise tape and concrete objects. All other sounds were made with two sine/square-wave oscillators. A number of superimpositions were required at 5, 6, and 24. The staccato melodic shapes were obtained by altering the frequency, followed by a quick increase of volume from zero, and many repetitions of the process. The final recording of this section was at double speed. Obviously a synthesizer would simplify the task.

MORE NEW SOUNDS—6

VOICE AND MAGNETIC TAPE

GEORGE SELF

135